The Gambler's Guide to Taxes

THE GAMBLER'S GUIDE TO TAXES

How to Keep More of
What You Win

WALTER L. LEWIS, CPA

A Lyle Stuart Book
Kensington Publishing Corporation
www.kensingtonbooks.com

LYLE STUART BOOKS are published by

Kensington Publishing Corp.
850 Third Avenue
New York, NY 10022

All Kensington titles, imprints, and distributed lines are available at special quantity discounts for bulk purchases for sales promotions, premiums, fund-raising, educational, or institutional use. Special book excerpts or customized printings can also be created to fit specific needs. For details, write or phone the office of the Kensington special sales manager: Kensington Publishing Corp., 850 Third Avenue, New York, NY 10022, attn: Special Sales Department; phone: 1-800-221-2647.

Lyle Stuart is a trademark of Kensington Publishing Corp.

First printing: July 2003

10 9 8 7 6 5 4 3 2 1

Printed in the United States of America

ISBN 0-8184-0632-1

Dedicated to the memory of Walter and Laura Lewis, who encouraged me to take a chance, roll the dice, and always make the best out of the hand life dealt me.

Contents

Part I
THE GUIDE

Part II
SELECTED ARTICLES

Part III
USEFUL INFORMATION PUBLISHED BY THE INTERNAL REVENUE SERVICE

Conclusion   149

References and Resources   150

Index   153

About the Author   160

Acknowledgments

Thanks to my wife, Suzanne, for being my initial sounding board and helping with the original text.

Thanks to my daughter, Sara Witmer, for taking the time to type and retype the manuscript.

Thanks to the following, who contributed articles that have become an important part of this book:

I. NELSON ROSE

Professor I. Nelson Rose is an internationally known public speaker, writer, and scholar, and is recognized as one of the world's leading authorities on gambling law. He is a tenured full professor at Whittier Law School in Costa Mesa, California, and the author of more than 300 articles and books, including his internationally syndicated column and landmark 1986 book *Gambling and the Law*. His most recent books are *The Law of Internet Gambling* (Mary Ann Liebert Publishers 2002), and as coauthor, *Blackjack and the Law* (RGE Publishing 1998), and *Gaming Law Cases and Materials* (Lexis Publishing 2002). Professor Rose has testified as an expert witness and acted as a consultant to government and industry, including international corporations, major law firms, licensed casinos, Indian tribes, lottery operators and suppliers, and local, state, and national governments such as those of Arizona, California, Florida, Illinois, New Jersey, Texas, the province of Ontario, and the federal governments of Canada and the United States.

I. Nelson Rose, Professor of Law, Whittier Law School
Home Office: 17031 Encino Hills Drive, Encino, California 91436
(818) 788-8509; fax: (818) 788-3104

Web site: www.GamblingAndTheLaw.com
E-mail: rose@sprintmail.com

ROY A. LEWIS, E.A.

Roy A. Lewis, E.A., has offices in Tempe, Arizona, and Lake Arrowhead, California, and has been providing tax planning and preparation services to his clients throughout the United States since 1978. He received his undergraduate degree in 1974 from California State University-Fullerton and did his graduate work at CSU-Long Beach.

BASIL NESTOR

Basil Nestor is author of the *Unofficial Guide to Casino Gambling,* the comprehensive handbook that teaches players how to avoid sucker bets and beat casinos at their own games. He is also a feature writer and columnist for *Casino Player* magazine.

KAY BELL

Kay Bell has spent fifteen years of her professional life focusing on tax policy. That interest and expertise led her in 1999 to Bankrate. com, where she helped launch the Web site's tax coverage to complement its other financial stories. At Bankrate, Bell follows federal tax legislation, state tax developments, and writes consumer-oriented tax stories, with a focus on often-overlooked tax moves that can save taxpayers money.

Before joining the Florida-based Bankrate, Bell lived in the metro–D.C. area where she was a member of the government relations team for two large companies (Nestle, USA and steel company LTV) with emphasis on tax and trade matters. Prior to joining the private sector in Washington, Bell was a staffer with the tax-writing U.S. House Ways and Means Committee. Her first Capitol Hill position was as legislative assistant to a congressman who served on Ways and Means, and she stayed with his office when he subsequently was elected to the U.S. Senate.

Bell began her writing career twenty-five years ago in her native Texas, where she joined the staff of the Lubbock *Avalanche-Journal*, the south plains largest daily newspaper, while completing her bachelor's degree in journalism at Texas Tech University. After graduation, she moved from the paper's wire room to its reporting staff and within three years was named assistant city editor for A-J's morning edition.

She is married to fellow writer/editor John P. Holmes and lives in Palm Beach Gardens, Florida.

A. J. COOK

A. J. Cook, now practicing as a tax lawyer, is counsel with the law firm of Pietrangelo Cook PLC. Cook was formerly with the big-five CPA firm Ernst & Young as a partner in charge of tax services. Cook started writing his column, "A. J.'s Tax Fables," in 1983. It is now published in newspapers throughout the U.S. Archives of his column are at www.taxfables.com.

TOM STAMATSON

Tom Stamatson began sweeping in the early '80s—acutally his wife began then, and Tom laughed at her—until she won $6,000. When online sweeps began, she was right in there with the first win in 1986. She worked at About.com and when the contests and sweepstakes site became available, she urged Tom to apply. The rest is history . . .

JAMES W. CRAWFORD, CPA

James W. Crawford, CPA, founded the firm James W. Crawford, CPA in 1972. The firm is located in Monroe, Louisiana. James earned his bachelor of science degree in business administration from the University of Louisiana at Monroe and has done graduate studies toward an MBA degree at Tulane University.

Finally, thanks to a special group of individuals whose adventures convinced me of the need for this book.

Warning—Disclaimer

It should be understood that neither the author nor the publisher of this book are engaged in any way in providing legal, accounting, tax, or other professional services. This book has been published in order to provide our readers with accurate, authoritative information that they can then use to supplement, complement, and amplify other existing information that is available about gaming and taxes. We advise you to read and study as many of these materials as you can and urge you to consult with a legal, accounting, or tax professional in regard to any questions you may have about your own taxes or gambling winnings and losses.

This book is to be used as a general guide and source of background information about gambling and taxes. We hope that it will help you to plan wisely and to avoid some common tax-liability pitfalls. We do not, however, suggest, imply, or recommend in any way that readers can use this book to avoid paying taxes that they legally owe. The information contained herein is meant to help you become more familiar with the laws as they are and how to obey and use them wisely. It should also be understood that the information given will be outdated if tax laws or regulations change after the printing date.

The publishers and author recognize revenue procedures and tax forms are in the public domain. However, their arrangement and compilation along with the other material in this guide are subject to the copyright notice. The purpose of the book is to entertain and educate our readers. The author and publishers shall have neither responsibility nor liability to any person or entity with respect to any loss or damage caused, or alleged to be caused, directly or indirectly by the information contained in this book.

Your questions, comments, and suggestions are welcomed by the author, and can be mailed to him at this address: Walter L. Lewis, CPA, 1776 Warren Road, Indiana, PA 15701.

Introduction

To gamble legally in the United States between 1910 and 1930, one had to go to racetracks in Maryland or Kentucky. During the Depression, Nevada relegalized gambling and other states allowed wagering at racetracks. In 1964, New Hampshire held the first state lottery. Today, more people are gambling than ever before, and both the numbers of gamblers and the amount of their wagers are expected to grow. All but two states now have some form of legalized gambling, and it is appearing in many new environments: on Indian reservations, riverboats, the Internet, and on international air flights.

The Internal Revenue Service (IRS) is well aware of this increase in activity. For the IRS, this increase is a win-win situation. More players mean there will be more taxable winnings. Casinos annually issue more than 5.3 million Form W-2Gs to winners. Since losses can be deducted only to the extent of the winnings, the IRS has no fear of having to give back any tax dollars to losers. By enforcing strict regulations to substantiate losses and creating additional tax liability even after deducting those losses, the IRS looks at gamblers as a large potential source of new tax revenue.

This guide contains:

- Answers to thirty of the most frequently asked questions related to the tax treatment of gambling winnings and losses.
- Easy to follow, step-by-step instructions on how to report your gambling winnings and losses.
- Reproduction of many useful documents published by the Internal Revenue Service.
- A selection of articles written by a variety of gambling and tax experts.

Gambling winnings and losses can significantly impact your tax liability and your obligation to properly report your income. Information contained in this document is, in most cases, very general. After reading it you are advised to discuss your personal situation with your tax consultant.

Part I

THE GUIDE

1

◆

Don't Be a
"Louie the Loser"

Wally the Winner and Louie the Loser are the best of friends. They do many things together, but their recreation-of-choice is gambling.

Casinos and the tracks are their favorites, and although they go there together, their style of play is almost totally different.

At the track, Wally studies the program and handicaps the horses before making his wager. Louie sits at the bar until a minute before post time, then runs to the window and bets on a hunch.

When the evening is over, Wally saves his tickets and records his winnings and losses in his gambling journal. Louie rips up his losers, cusses, blames the jockeys, and swears he'll never come back (until the next time anyway).

On trips to the casinos, Wally sticks to a system and plays within controlled limits. As always, he finishes his session by documenting the evening's activities. Louie, on the other hand, sits at the blackjack table and bets erratically. Sometimes hitting sixteen when the dealer shows a face card, sometimes not. Sometimes hitting thirteen when the dealer shows a six, sometimes not. On rare occasions, he actually wins, and proclaims himself "The Greatest Blackjack Player of All Time." Louie finally leaves before the other players have him removed from the table. He decides to join the fun at the craps table.

There, he jumps between the pass and don't pass line, makes mostly the wrong choices, and blames the shooter. Within a short period of time, Louie leaves, much to the relief of the other players.

At the end of the day, Wally meets Louie at the buffet. Wally listens to Louie's tales of woe, hears about how close Louie came to breaking even and how he knows his luck is going to change. Louie also tells Wally about all the new friends he met while playing. Wally usually picks up the check since Louie is almost always broke.

At the end of the year, Wally tallies his winnings at $10,000 with documented losses of $8,000.

Louie has no clue how much he lost during the year, but guesses it to be around $18,000. Since he hasn't kept a journal, there is no way for him to know for sure.

For Louie, when it comes to gambling and taxes, Murphy's Law prevails. On New Year's Eve, Wally has a date. Louie must make their annual trip to the casinos to bet and to watch the college bowl games by himself.

As Louie enters his first casino, he decides to do something different—kill some time at the slot machines. He searches for a machine that he knows is "ready to hit," throws in three silver dollars, and something astounding happens! He hits . . . BIG TIME! Bells ring, sirens scream, and lights flash.

Casino officials rush over to congratulate him and arrange his payout—$20,000. Louie won $20,000!

The first thing they do is ask him to sign Form W-2G, which they are required by law to send to the Internal Revenue Service. Already shocked, Louie is now in a panic. He begs and pleads with them not to tell the IRS about his win, but there is nothing they can do. It's the law.

Louie now thinks of his buddy Wally and all the time he spent documenting his gambling activity—winnings and losses—and wonders where his first big win will leave him with the IRS.

He will now be on record with the IRS as a $20,000 winner. The only loss he could document is the $3.00 he played to win the $20,000.

Had he kept a journal, Louie could have deducted his $18,000 in losses. But, you guessed it, the IRS now considers him to be a $19,997 winner and will tax him accordingly.

Louie is a loser. Wally is a winner because *Wally read this book*.

The moral of the story: Don't gamble unless you are prepared to win.

2

◆

Questions and Answers

1. **What types of activities are included in reportable gambling winnings?**
Reportable gambling winnings include, but are not limited to, lotteries, bingo, raffles, horse and dog racing, and all casino activities.

2. **Am I responsible to report only the winnings that have been reported to me by the gambling establishment?**
No. You must report all winnings. The diary you keep (see question 13) must document all winnings and losses.

3. **By "all winnings" do you mean just winnings from legal activities?**
No. All winnings include winnings from both legal and illegal activities.

4. **How do I report my gambling winnings?**
Gambling winnings are reported on Form 1040, line 21 of the U.S. Individual Income Tax Return as other income "Gambling."

5. **Can I write off my gambling losses?**
You may write off your substantiated gambling losses to the ex-

tent of your gambling winnings on Schedule A—Itemized Deductions as an "Other Miscellaneous Deduction."

6. I itemize deductions and am able to substantiate more losses than winnings. May I deduct the excess losses?
No. Substantiated losses are deductible only to the extent of gambling winnings.

7. I file a joint return with my spouse. I had substantial documented losses in 2002, while my spouse had gambling winnings. May we combine our winnings and losses on our 2002 tax return?
Yes. If a husband and wife file a joint return, they may combine substantiated losses and deduct to the extent of both spouses' winnings.

8. In 2002, I won money playing blackjack, lost money playing the state lottery, and lost money betting on the horses. Do I have to report each activity individually?
No. Losses from one type of gambling activity may be offset against gains from another type of gambling activity. However, separate reporting of each gambling activity should be documented in your diary.

9. In 2001, I had gambling losses that exceeded gambling winnings by a substantial amount. In 2002 my gambling winnings exceeded my gambling losses. May I use the unused portion of my 2001 losses to offset my 2002 winnings?
No. Gambling losses can only be used to offset gambling winnings during the same year. Excess gambling losses may not be carried forward or carried back to any other tax year.

10. If I have gambling losses equal to or greater than my gambling winnings, there will be no effect on my tax liability because one will offset the other. Is this right?
Not necessarily.
First, you need to have proper substantiation for the losses you are claiming (see question 13). Without appropriate documentation, losses could be disallowed by the IRS.

Next, you must itemize deductions in order to claim your losses. You will only itemize your deductions if they exceed the standard deduction amount. For 2002 the standard deduction amount for a single taxpayer is $4,700. For a married couple filing a joint return the amount is $7,850.

Finally, by including winnings in gross income on Form 1040, your adjusted gross income amount could impact many calculations you may be subject to. As an example:

- If you receive social security benefits, a larger dollar amount may be taxable.
- If you itemize deductions and have deductible medical expenses, a smaller dollar amount will be deductible
- If you itemize deductions and have deductible job related and other miscellaneous expenses, a smaller amount will be deductible.
- If you itemize deductions, a smaller amount of the total may be deductible.
- You could have your personal exemption deduction lowered or lose the entire amount.
- If you claim the Child Tax Credit, the amount could be phased out.
- If you qualify for either the Hope or the Lifetime Learning education credits, they may be reduced or eliminated.
- Less of your student-loan interest may be deducted.
- You may no longer be entitled to a deduction for your traditional IRA.
- You may not be eligible to make a Roth IRA contribution.

11. **I know my gambling losses far exceed my gambling winnings. If I include my winnings in gross income, and losses as an itemized deduction to the extent of the winnings, will I be challenged by the IRS?**
You could be, just as you could be challenged by the IRS for any of the items on your return. However, if you have reported all of your winnings and have the proper documentation to support your losses, you will feel more comfortable answering any questions the IRS may ask you.

12. **Will the IRS accept my gambling losses if they do not exceed my gambling winnings?**
Your gambling losses must be substantiated with adequate documentary evidence if you are challenged by the IRS.

13. **Will the IRS accept my statement that my gambling losses exceed my gambling winnings?**
No. There are guidelines recommended in Revenue Procedure 77-29 that should be followed to substantiate losses (see Chapter Six).

14. **What is Revenue Procedure 77-29?**
Revenue Procedure 77-29 provides taxpayers with guidelines concerning the treatment of both gambling winnings and losses and the responsibility for maintaining adequate documentation of winnings and losses. This procedure is reprinted in Chapter Six.

15. **I did not report my gambling winnings and losses in 2001. What should I do?**
You have three years to file Form 1040X and amend the information contained in your original return. If you filed your 2001 tax return by April 15, 2002, you have until April 15, 2005 to file an amendment (see example in Chapter Eleven).

16. **Do I have to report my winnings from gambling in a foreign country, on a cruise ship, or from playing a foreign lottery or sweepstakes?**
Yes, you are taxed on your worldwide income unless specifically exempted by the Internal Revenue Code. Gambling winnings that occur outside the United States are not exempted.

17. **Are you sure the IRS won't permit me to offset my losses against my winnings and report the net amount?**
Yes, I am sure. Many court cases address this point. Also, the tax booklet included with Form 1040 mailed to taxpayers includes, as part of the instructions of line 21:

Gambling winnings, including lotteries, raffles, a lump sum payment from the sale of a right to receive future lottery payments, etc., are gambling winnings. You must report the full amount of your winnings on line 21. You cannot offset losses against winnings and report the difference. If you had any gambling losses, you may take them as an itemized deduction on Schedule A. But, you cannot deduct more than the winnings you report.

18. **As a recreational gambler, are my winnings subject to self-employment taxes?**
No, gambling winnings are not considered earned income unless you are a professional gambler (see Chapter Four).

19. **A group of us from the office went together and bought a lottery ticket. We won an amount in excess of the minimum required for a W-2G to be issued. Who decides the taxpayer's name in which the form will be issued?**
A designated member from the group must request a Form 5754. On this form all the winners will be identified for the purpose of issuing the W-2G (see Chapter Seven).

20. **How detailed must I be in reporting winnings and losses? Must I sit with my diary and record every pull I make on the slot machine, every hand of blackjack, every race on which I place a bet, or every game of bingo? This will take all the fun out of gambling!**
The Tax Court, in various decisions, has considered the recording of winnings and losses and tried to give guidance in the areas of what is practical. In *Szkirczak v. Commissioner*, the Tax Court noted it was impractical to record each separate roll of the dice or spin of the wheel. In the same case, they allowed offsetting of winnings and losses by the game. In *Winkler v. U.S.*, they allowed netting by the race, and in *Green v. Commissioner*, they allowed netting by the day. Revenue Procedure 77-29 specifically addresses the following six types of gambling:

Keno—The Procedure indicates keeping "copies of tickets purchased by the taxpayer and validated by the gambling establishment." No reference in this section addresses how often wins must be recorded. Because of the similarities to bingo, those guidelines could be followed.

Slot Machines—The Procedure indicates keeping "a record of all winnings by date and time that the machine was played." It does not seem reasonable the IRS intends every pull to be recorded. The activity should be summarized for the time spent on the machine for a particular day.

Table Games—The Procedure indicates maintaining a record of "the number of the table at which the taxpayer was playing." The implication is that gambling activity (win/loss) should be reported when leaving each table. This section applies to blackjack, craps, poker, baccarat, roulette, etc.

Bingo—The Procedure indicates keeping "a record of the number of games played, cost of the tickets purchased and amounts collected on winning tickets." Since most bingo games have a starting time and an ending time, it is reasonable to assume the IRS would only require one record for that particular date.

Racing: Horses, Harness, Dog, etc.—The Procedure indicates "a record of the races, entries, amounts of wagers, and amounts collected on winning tickets and amounts lost on losing tickets should be kept." From this it is assumed that each race must be reported separately.

Lotteries—The Procedure indicates keeping "a record of ticket purchases, dates, winnings, and losses." The amount of each winning ticket should be recorded. All losing tickets should be kept and recorded.

21. **How are lottery winnings reported?**
Lottery, sweepstake, and raffle winnings are reported in the same way as other gambling winnings. They are included as "other income" on line 21 of Form 1040. Substantiated losses (the cost of lottery, sweepstake, or raffle tickets) are deductible to the extent of reported winnings only if you itemize deductions.

22. **How are installment payments of lottery winnings reported?**
Currently, if winnings are payable in installments, you report as "other income" on line 21 of Form 1040 the amount you receive each year.

23. **Are deductions allowed for gambling losses against installment payments of lottery winnings?**

Yes, installment payments of lottery winnings maintain their characteristic as gambling winnings. Substantiated gambling losses, incurred in the current year, to the extent of the winnings are deductible if you itemize deductions.

24. **What difference does it make if one person reports the entire amount of a lottery jackpot or it is split among a number of people?**

The tax advantage of splitting a lottery prize can be significant. So significant that the IRS will not allow the prize to be split after it is won. IRS Form 5754 (see Forms to the Gambler—Chapter Seven) is used to report a group of winners on the same ticket.

The following example will clearly present the advantage of splitting a lottery prize:

Sara buys a lottery ticket and wins $300,000. To keep the example as simple as possible, we will assume her taxable income is $300,000. Sara's federal tax liability (for the year 2002) would be $92,253.

   Sara, Anne, and Shannon jointly buy a lottery ticket and win $300,000 ($100,000 each). Again, to keep the example as simple as possible, we will assume each person's taxable income is $100,000. Each would have a federal tax liability (for the year 2002) of $24,315. The total tax liability on the $300,000 would be $72,945. This is $19,308 less than the tax to Sara alone. The larger the prize, and/or the more taxpayers that share the prize, the larger the overall savings. The reason the tax liability is less if the income is divided among a number of taxpayers is the graduated nature of the federal tax structure. For the year 2002 the tax rates for a single taxpayer are:

TAXABLE INCOME

Is Between		Your tax is:		Of the amount over
$0	$6,000		+10%	$0
$6,000	$27,950	$600	+15%	$6,000
$27,950	$67,700	$3,893	+27%	$27,950
$67,700	$141,250	$14,625	+30%	$67,700
$141,250	$307,050	$36,690	+35%	$141,250
$307,050	—	$94,720	+38.6%	$307,050

25. I work in a casino as a dealer and do a small amount of recreational gambling. Can I combine my gambling winnings with the tips or tokes I receive as a dealer?

Tips or tokes received by you as a gaming employee in connection with your employment must be included in gross income. However, tips are not gains from wagering transactions against which gambling losses may be deducted.

26. I enjoy betting on the horses. Would it be wise for me to structure my bets to avoid or limit the amount reported to me on Form W-2G?

Nice try, but the answer is no for two reasons. First, you must report all gambling winnings, not just those reported on Form W-2G. Second, you may have to give the payer a statement of the amount of your winnings, if any, from identical wagers. If this statement is required, the payer will ask you for it. You provide this statement by signing Form W-2G, or if required, Form 5754.

Identical wagers include two bets placed in a pari-mutuel pool on one horse to win a particular race. However, the bets are not identical if one bet is "to win" and one bet is "to place." In addition, they are not identical if the bets were placed in different pari-mutuel pools. For example, a bet in a pool conducted by the racetrack and a bet in a separate pool conducted by an off-track betting establishment in which the bets are not pooled with those placed at the track are not identical wagers.

27. I sold my rights to receive payments over a number of years on a lottery winning. Can I continue to report the amount I was entitled to over the same number of years?

No, you must report the entire amount you received in the year it was received.

28. Last year I won a car during a special promotion a casino was running. The casino offered me $25,000 or the vehicle. I left with the vehicle. The casino gave me a W-2G showing the winnings as $25,000. During the same year I sold the car for

$20,000. Must I report the $25,000, or can I only report the amount I sold it for?

The Internal Revenue Code requires that all noncash winnings be reported at the fair market value. You indicated the casino offered you $25,000 and since you elected to receive the car the fair market value has been established at $25,000.

29. **I am a resident of Canada and frequently visit the casinos in the United States. Last year I won a jackpot on a slot machine. The win was large enough for tax to be withheld. Can I get this money refunded to me?**

You may be able to get some, if not all, of the money back. Here is the procedure to follow:

1. Complete Form W-7 to apply for a US Individual Taxpayer Identification Number (ITIN). This number is similar to a social security number. The application can be obtained from any IRS office or from the IRS Web site.
2. Complete the Form 1040NR. This is a nonresident individual income tax return.
3. You may be able to deduct your substantiated losses against the amount you won. See Chapters Six and Eight in this book to learn how to substantiate and deduct your losses.

30. **What are the reporting requirements for cash transactions?**

Cash transactions in a casino are reported on Form 8362-Currency Transactions Report by Casinos. A casino must file Form 8362 for each transaction involving either currency received (Cash In) or currency disbursed (Cash Out) of more than $10,000 in a gaming day. Multiple transactions must be treated as a single transaction if the casino has knowledge that: (1) they are made by or on behalf of the same person, and (2) they result in either Cash In or Cash Out by the casino totaling more than $10,000 during any one gaming day. Reportable transactions may occur at a casino cage, gaming table, and/or slot machine.

3

◆

Seven and Out for the IRS

It is common knowledge that casinos, under certain circumstances, provide lodging, food, beverages, entertainment, or recreational activities without charge ("comps") to select patrons. Casinos provide these benefits to induce the gamblers to patronize their casino. Comps are usually issued taking into account the patron's average bet, the time spent gambling, the number of hands played per hour, and a factor to reflect the fact that the odds are in the casino's favor.

A CASE STUDY

Robert LiButti, a horse broker from New Jersey, gambled extensively in Atlantic City, New Jersey, during the years 1987, 1988, and 1989. In 1987, he spent eighty-four days at the casino and gambled on seventy-five of the days with an average bet of approximately $15,000. During 1988, he spent 179 days at the casino gambling on 148 of the days with an average bet of approximately $11,500. In 1989 he spent 304 days at the casino and gambled on seventy of the days with an average bet of approximately $9,225. He played mostly craps and had losses of $4,139,100 in 1987, $3,080,050 in 1988, and $1,215,900 in 1989.

During this period, the casino issued various comps to Robert Li-Butti and annually sent him Form 1099 Miscellaneous Income reporting their value. The comps were for more than a room at the casino and a trip to the buffet. The comps included five Rolls Royces ($913,300), three Ferraris ($731,400), one Bentley Corniche ($212,000), one Mercedes Benz ($60,583), five European vacations ($87,840), a Rolex watch and bracelet ($32,300), a 2.7 karat diamond ($30,000), and 178 bottles of Cristal Rose ($40,050). The 1099 issued by the casino to Robert LiButti indicated taxable income for 1987, 1988, and 1989 in the amounts of $443,278, $974,992 and $1,126,856, respectively.

The Taxpayer

Robert LiButti lost a substantial amount of money gambling, and received a substantial amount of value in comps. On his federal tax return, he included the value of the comps in his gross income and relied on Section 165(d) to deduct an equal amount of his gambling losses. His position was that comps are a part of "gains from wagering transactions" and therefore, the deduction for the losses was appropriate.

The IRS

The IRS disagreed. In their notice to LiButti dated November 12, 1992, they stated that gambling losses are allowed only to the extent they offset gains from wagering. They claimed that income received from the casino in the form of comps cannot be treated as gains from wagering transactions pursuant to Internal Revenue Code Section 165 (d). In other words, they thought LiButti underpaid his taxes. They issued substantial income tax deficiency notices and assessed additional amounts for various penalties.

The Tax Court Rules

LiButti's case was submitted to the Court without trial. LiButti petitioned the Court for a redetermination of his income tax liability. The question facing the Court was whether LiButti could deduct gambling losses to the extent of the value of the "complementary goods and services" he received from the casino.

The Court recognized the fact that gambling is a multibillion-dollar industry and has become a major source of adult entertainment. In an effort to attract and retain patrons, casinos offer comps. The Court also addressed the issue of whether the comps were actually free of charge. As always, with the IRS, the taxpayer bears the burden of proof.

The Court agreed that LiButti is entitled to deduct his losses from wagering transactions to the extent of the gains from such transactions. Since neither the Internal Revenue Service Code nor the regulations define the phrase "gains from such transactions," the Court looked to *Webster's New World Dictionary* for help with the definition of "gain." It found the definition to include "an increase in wealth, earnings, etc.; profit; winnings." After reviewing other court cases that tried to define the meaning of "gains from such transactions," the Court discovered that the term has sometimes been equated directly with gambling winnings.

The comps from the casino increased LiButti's wealth and were a direct result of his gambling at the casino. The Court recognized the fact that had LiButti not gambled extensively at the casino, he would not have received the comps. The Court also addressed the issue that LiButti's receipt of the comps did not directly hinge on his success or failure in the casino.

The Court agreed with LiButti that "gains from such transactions" can include gambling winnings. Although "winnings" is one of the definitions of gains, it is certainly not the only definition. "Increases in wealth" is another viable meaning of the term, and the Court felt that LiButti's wealth was increased by the comps. It stated that had Congress wanted to limit the definition of "gains," it would have used the term "winnings." The Court ruled in favor of LiButti and allowed the losses to the extent of gains to include the value of the comps.

The Conclusion

As the gaming industry expands and the number of gamblers at the level of LiButti increases, this case will have more significance. For the gambler that loses $1,000 but receives a 1099 for $600 (minimum value at which a 1099 must be issued) worth of hotel room and meal value, he/she can use this case to deduct $600 of the losses.

Once again, the importance of proper documentation of losses is evident. Without it, the possibility of paying tax on what was thought to be a free room or meal becomes reality.

4

◆

The Professional Gambler

Professional gamblers are considered to be in the business of gambling. This occupational classification had been reviewed in many Tax Court cases over the years and there is now adequate precedent to help determine who qualifies as a professional gambler. The basic qualifying criteria are the same as those used to determine if any activity is a hobby or a true business venture. These qualifications include:

- There must be a profit motive. The expectation of making a profit to be able to support oneself must be evident. A profit must be shown in at least three of the last five years.
- A considerable amount of time must be spent gambling. Gambling must be done with regularity.
- A business operation must be evident. The IRS requires all businesses to maintain a set of books and records that document the activity. Other items that would indicate business intentions include business cards, letterhead or stationery, all required business licenses and registrations, a business telephone listing, and an office address or post office box.

TAX TIME

The tax reporting of a professional gambler is different from that of a recreational gambler. A recreational gambler can report losses only to the extent of gains from gambling activity. The recreational gambler reports gains as part of adjusted gross income and may report losses only if deductions are itemized.

The professional gambler is not required to report losses as an itemized deduction. Instead, losses and gains are reported on Schedule C. The net gain or loss is then reported on Form 1040 prior to arriving at adjusted gross income. This should cause the professional gambler's adjusted gross income to be much lower than that of the recreational gambler. The significance of the adjusted gross income, in determining the taxability of social security benefits, has been addressed in Chapter Ten of this guide. Be aware that adjusted gross income also affects certain tax credits, the alternative minimum tax, limitations on itemized deductions, and limitations on the exemption deduction.

The professional gambler is able to deduct necessary and ordinary business expenses from gambling gains.

Deductible expenses on Schedule C include:

Travel expenses
Meals and entertainment (with limitation)
Licenses and permits
Office supplies
Legal and professional services
Insurance
Dues and publications
Books, journals, seminars, and conferences
Other gambling-related items

All deductions must be considered ordinary and necessary for the conduct of the business activity.

Finally, the net income calculated on Schedule C is subject to self-employment tax. The self-employment tax is a two-tier tax calculated on Schedule SE. The first tier is the Social Security amount that is based on the first $84,900 of net income at a rate of 12.4 percent. The second portion is the Medicare calculation at a rate of 2.9 percent on the total net income.

GAMBLERS IN COURT

There are many Tax Court cases that addressed the issue of whether or not an individual was a professional gambler. Prior to 1985, gamblers had difficulty establishing gambling as a profession or full-time occupation. They were unable to overcome a long-standing precedent that defined carrying on a trade or business as holding oneself out to others engaged in the selling of goods and services. The following two cases are examples of unsuccessful attempts to establish a professional-gambler status.

In the case of the *Estate of Dan B. Cull* v. *Commissioner of Internal Revenue*, the issue of whether a full-time gambler for his own account was engaged in a "trade or business" within the meaning of the Internal Revenue Code was addressed.

During the year being audited, Mr. Cull was a full-time parimutuel clerk at various racetracks. He placed wagers almost daily. When Mr. Cull was not working, he was gathering information to assist him in placing bets. He would arrive at the tracks early enough to question owners, trainers, and jockeys. Toward the end of the year, he took a number of days off from his full-time job in order to devote the entire day to betting.

Mr. Cull gambled only with his own money for his own account. He maintained a detailed ledger in which he recorded his wagering activity on each race.

Using *Gentile* v. *Commissioner*, 65 T.C. 1 (1975) as a precedent, which defined "carrying on a trade or business" as holding oneself out to others as engaged in the selling of goods and services, the Court ruled that Mr. Cull was not in a trade or business.

This test was also used in the case of *Louis and Ann Noto* v. *United States* in the District Court of New Jersey. In this case, the Court did not dispute the fact that for the year in question, Louis Noto devoted a substantial amount of time and effort to gambling. He maintained records of his gambling winnings and losses along with the daily racing forms he used. All of his gambling was for his own benefit. He used his own money for the wagers and at no time did he place bets for others or hold himself out to be a horse race consultant. The Court ruled that without the offering of "goods or services," the taxpayer was not in a trade or business.

Finally, a case was presented that resulted in a favorable ruling for the gambler and established a precedent for gamblers to file their tax returns as being in a trade or business. The details of this case, involving Robert P. Groetzinger, are presented on the following pages.

Robert P. Groetzinger was involved on a full-time basis in pari-mutuel wagering on dog races. He had no other professional income or employment during the 1978 tax year (the year in question). Groetzinger went to the track from 1:00 P.M. to 11:30 P.M., six days a week, and spent a substantial amount of time preparing to make his wagers. Groetzinger never placed bets for others or received fees for selling tips.

On his 1978 tax return, Groetzinger reported his gambling activity on Schedule E, Supplemental Income Schedule. The activity included $72,032 of bets placed and $70,000 of winnings. He did not deduct his $2,032 net gambling loss in arriving at his adjusted gross income.

The IRS took the position that the $70,000 of winnings constituted income from gambling and had to be reported as miscellaneous income on his Form 1040. He could then deduct $70,000 as a miscellaneous itemized deduction on Schedule A. The IRS calculated an alternative minimum tax due of $2,142.

The issue to be addressed by the Tax Court was whether the "goods and services" test should be an absolute prerequisite to a finding that a taxpayer is engaged in a "trade or business." The Tax Court reviewed many prior rulings that focused on the issue of what constitutes a "trade or business." It concluded that the term "trade or business" should have a broad interpretation. It determined that there was no basis for distinguishing between different types of occupations in determining whether a person is engaged in a trade or business. It did not limit the definition to include only industrial or commercial activities, but also professionals such as athletes and artists. After agreeing on what was included in "trade or business," the case became an easy one. The Tax Court agreed that Groetzinger devoted a substantial amount of time to his gambling efforts with the intent to earn a living from the activity. The ruling, in this case, was that the evidence supported Groetzinger's position that his gambling activities constituted a "trade or business."

On August 21, 1985, the United States Court of Appeals for the Seventh Circuit agreed with the Tax Court decision. The Groetzinger case set the precedent for professional gamblers to deduct gambling losses from gambling gains prior to arriving at adjusted gross income.

PROFESSIONAL OR RECREATIONAL

For the gambler, there is no set answer to the question "Is it better to file as a recreational or professional gambler?" The facts and circumstances of each particular situation ultimately determine the filing status.

The differences between filing as a recreational versus a professional gambler include:

- The recreational gambler reports all winnings as income and deducts losses as an itemized deduction. The professional gambler has the opportunity to net his losses against his winnings on Schedule C and report the difference on his Form 1040.
- The lowest adjusted gross income amount on Form 1040 will be achieved by the professional gambler.
- The professional gambler will be subject to Social Security and Medicare taxes on his net income from gambling.
- The professional gambler may establish one of many available retirement accounts with the potential of deferring substantial amounts of earned income.
- The professional gambler may deduct expenses that are ordinary and necessary and that are directly related to the gambling activity.

Remember, professional and recreational gamblers have the same burden of proof to substantiate their gambling winnings and losses. A gambling journal or diary is required in either case.

5

◆

I Won, I Won, I Won

Once the initial excitement of winning has subsided, the realization of having to deal with the IRS will come. There are tax strategies that you should review to make certain you "Keep More of What You Win." After all, the less you give to the IRS, the more you get to keep.

THE DIARY

A review of the current year's gambling diary must be made to ensure that it will substantiate the amount of winnings and losses being claimed. In years in which no gains or losses are reported, there is no need for the IRS to question the information in the diary. The year with an obvious reportable win, there is greater likelihood that the information in the diary will be questioned. Make sure the diary is complete, up-to-date, and all available supporting documentation is in order.

REDUCE ADJUSTED GROSS INCOME

The federal income taxing system is based on a series of graduated tax rates. The higher the taxable income, the higher the tax rate. The current rates range from 10 percent to 38.6 percent on ordinary income (not including capital gains rates). To avoid gambling winnings from being taxed at a higher rate than the gambler is accustomed to, other types of income should be deferred to next year if possible. A review of all income sources should be made to determine if there is any flexibility in deciding when to receive the income. Self-employed taxpayers may have more opportunities to defer income than wage earners. Some self-employed individuals will want to review the possibility of increasing contributions to retirement programs, while wage earners will want to review increasing amounts deducted for 401(K) or tax-sheltered annuity plans or other available tax-deferral programs. Contributions to Individual Retirement Accounts for both the gambler and the spouse may provide an additional opportunity to reduce adjusted gross income.

INCREASE ITEMIZED DEDUCTIONS

Remember, for the recreational gambler, gambling losses may be taken only if itemized deductions are claimed. Itemized deductions will be claimed only if they exceed the standard deduction amount. An example: A married couple filing a joint return normally claims the standard deduction of $7,850 because their itemized deductions only total $3,000. This year they won $2,500 in the state lottery and have $2,500 of substantiated gambling losses. They will still claim the standard deduction since it is larger than their itemized deductions.

As a general rule, the larger the itemized deductions, the lower the taxable income. If this general rule were true in all cases, the strategy would be to accelerate as many of the itemized deductions into the current year from next year. The problem is that there are special provisions in the Internal Revenue Code that address the deductibility of itemized deductions. Medical and miscellaneous (union dues, tax preparation, certain unreimbursed employee expenses, etc.) deductions are limited to the amount that exceeds 7.5 percent of adjusted gross income for medical and 2 percent of adjusted gross income for miscellaneous. Since gambling gains increase adjusted gross income, it may be more difficult to deduct these types of expenses.

Therefore, it may be more beneficial to defer these expenses to next year, when the adjusted gross income could be less.

Other itemized deductions such as donations, certain taxes (such as real estate, state, and local taxes) and deductible interest should be reviewed for opportunities to accelerate amounts into the current year. However, an overall review of all itemized deductions should be made to determine if the limitations imposed once a certain level of adjusted gross income is attained will be in effect.

AVOID PENALTY AND INTEREST

No matter how much is owed to the IRS, when the tax return reporting the winnings is filed, penalty and interest should be avoided. The Internal Revenue Code requires taxes to be prepaid during the year through quarterly estimated payments or by having taxes withheld from salaries, wages, retirement payments, gambling winnings, and certain other amounts the taxpayer receives. To avoid owing penalty or interest, the amount prepaid must equal 90 percent of the current year's tax liability or 112 percent of the prior year's tax liability if the adjusted gross income for that year is more than $150,000. If the prior year's tax liability is less than the projection being made for the current year, there is an opportunity to hold on to some of the winnings for a longer period of time (possibly until April 15 of the following year). The calculation to determine the required prepayment amount is made on form 1040ES. To make this calculation, the following information is needed:

- A copy of the prior year's tax return.
- Projection of the current year's income.
- Projection of the amount of income tax that will be withheld from all sources including wages and gambling winnings.
- Projection of itemized deductions for the current year including gambling losses.

If the minimum amount that is required to be prepaid is properly calculated and paid, there will be no additional amounts due to cover unnecessary penalty and interest.

Time is very critical in each of the strategies mentioned above. The longer you wait, the fewer the number of options available. All tax-planning opportunities expire at year-end except the ability to contribute to an Individual Retirement Account and for the self-employed to contribute to a qualified retirement account.

6

◆

Substantiating Losses

If you don't keep a gambling diary, now is the time to start. The Internal Revenue Service issues Revenue Procedures on various subjects that affect the rights and duties of the taxpayers under the Internal Revenue Code. These procedures are considered to be matters of public knowledge. If gambling winnings and losses are claimed, the IRS will require compliance with the Revenue Procedures 77-29. The IRS has also issued Publication 529, "Miscellaneous Deductions," which includes a section on substantiating gambling losses.

WHAT THE IRS EXPECTS YOU TO KNOW

Revenue Procedure 77-29 provides guidelines concerning the proper treatment of wagering gains and losses for federal income tax purposes. More important, it discusses the taxpayers' responsibility for maintaining adequate records to support the claimed gains and losses. By providing these guidelines to the taxpayer, it also provides the IRS agent with guidelines to support the agent's claim that deductions should not be allowed.

YOUR GAMBLING DIARY

The IRS has not issued a preprinted format on which the taxpayer can fill in the blanks and be certain the information will, without question, be accepted. Therefore, knowledge of the information contained in Revenue Procedure 77-29 becomes extremely important. The Revenue Procedure requires a taxpayer to maintain, on a regular basis, an accurate diary, log, or similar record that is supported by appropriate evidence of both winnings and losses. Records should include:

- The type of gambling activity
- The date the activity took place
- Where the activity took place
- Who the taxpayer was with
- A statement of amount won and/or lost

Additional documented evidence of gambling winnings and losses could include appropriately dated:

- Airline or bus ticket to the gambling location
- Hotel charges
- Cash credit card advances
- Bank withdrawals
- Casino statement
- Racetrack program
- Unredeemed racetrack tickets
- Unredeemed lottery tickets

More specific guidelines for various gambling activities are presented in the Revenue Procedure that follows:

Revenue Procedure 77–29

Section 1: Purpose
The purpose of this revenue procedure is to provide guidelines to taxpayers concerning the treatment of wagering gains and losses for fed-

eral tax purposes and the related responsibility for maintaining adequate records in support of winnings and losses.

Section 2: Background

Income derived from wagering transactions is includible in gross income under the provisions of Section 61 of the Internal Revenue Code of 1954. Losses from wagering transactions are allowable only to the extent of gains from such transactions, under Section 165(d) of the Code, and may be claimed only as an itemized deduction.

Temporary regulations Section 7.66041-1 (T.D. 7492, 1977-2 C.B. 463) effective May 1, 1977, require all persons in a trade or business who, in the course of that trade or business, make any payment of $1,200 or more in winnings from a bingo game or slot machine play, or $1,500 or more in winnings from a keno game, to prepare Form W-2G, Statement for Certain Gambling Winnings, for each person to whom the winnings are paid. In determining whether such winnings equal or exceed the $1,500 reporting floor and in determining the amount to be reported on form W-2G in the case of a keno game, the amount of winnings from any one game shall be reduced by the amount wagered for that one game. In the case of bingo or slot machines, the total winnings will not be reduced by the amount wagered. Forms W-2G reporting such payments must be filed with the Internal Revenue Service on or before February 28 following the year of payment.

Winnings of $600 or more, unreduced by the amount of the wagers, must also be reported for every person paid gambling winnings from horse racing, or jai alai, if such winnings are at least 300 times the amount wagered.

Winnings of $600 or more, unreduced by the amount of the wagers, must also be reported for every person paid gambling winnings from state-conducted lotteries.

Under Section 6001 of the Code, the taxpayers must keep records necessary to verify items reported on their income tax returns. Records supporting items on a tax return should be retained until statute of limitations on that return expires.

Section 3: Procedures

An accurate diary or similar record regularly maintained by the tax-payer, supplemented by verifiable documentation, will usually be acceptable evidence for substantiation of wagering winnings and losses. In general, the diary should contain at least the following information:

1. Date and type of specific wager or wagering activity
2. Name of gambling establishment
3. Address or location of gambling establishment
4. Name(s) of other person(s) (if any) present with taxpayer at gambling establishment
5. Amount won or lost

Verifiable documentation for gambling transactions include, but is not limited to, Forms W-2G; Forms 5754, Statements by Person Receiving Gambling Winnings; wagering tickets; cancelled checks; credit records; bank withdrawals; and statements of actual winnings or payment slips provided to the taxpayer by the gambling establishment.

Where possible, the diary and available documentation generated with the placement and settlement of a wager should be further supported by other documentation of the taxpayer's wagering activity or visit to a gambling establishment. Such documentation includes, but is not limited to, hotel bills, airline tickets, gasoline credit cards, cancelled checks, credit records, bank deposits, and bank withdrawals.

Additional supporting evidence could also include affidavits or testimony from responsible gambling officials regarding wagering activity.

With regard to specific wagering transactions, winnings and losses may be further supported by the following items:

.01 **Keno**—Copies of keno tickets purchased by the taxpayer and validated by the gambling establishment, copies of the taxpayer's casino credit records, and copies of the taxpayer's casino check cashing records.

.02 **Slot Machines**—A record of all winnings by date and time that the machine was played. (In Nevada, the machine number is the number required by the State Gaming Commission and may or may not be displayed in a prominent place on the machine. If not displayed on the machine, the number may be requested from the casino's operator.)

.03 Table Games: Twenty one (Blackjack), Craps, Poker, Baccarat, Roulette, Wheel of Fortune, etc.—The number of the table at which the taxpayer was playing. Casino credit card data indicating whether the credit was issued in the pit or at the cashier's cage.

.04 Bingo—A record of the number of games played, cost of tickets purchased, and amounts collected on winning tickets. Supplemental records include any receipts from the casino, parlor, etc.

.05 Racing: Horses, Harness, Dog, etc.—A record of the races, entries, amounts of wagers, and amounts collected on winning tickets. Supplemental records include unredeemed tickets and payment records from the racetrack.

.06 Lotteries—A record of ticket purchases, dates, winnings, and losses. Supplemental records include unredeemed tickets, payment slips, and winnings statements.

The record-keeping suggestions set forth above are intended as general guidelines to assist taxpayers in establishing their reportable gambling gains and deductible gambling losses. While following these will enable most taxpayers to meet their obligations under the Internal Revenue Code, these guidelines cannot be all-inclusive and the tax liability of each depends on the facts and circumstances of particular situations.

The following forms were developed giving consideration to the guidelines in Revenue Procedure 77-29 and IRS Publication 529—"Miscellaneous Deductions." These forms may be copied and/or modified to record specific gambling activity.

Taxpayer's Name: _____

Taxpayer's Social Security Number: _____

Tax Year: _____

Date	Activity	Name of Establishment	Accompanied by	Machine Number	Amount Won	Amount Lost
	Slots					

Taxpayer's Name: _____

Taxpayer's Social Security Number: _____

Tax Year: _____

Date	Activity	Name of Establishment	Accompanied by	No. of Games	Cost of Ticket	Amount Won
	Bingo					

Supplemental information could include receipts obtained from the casino or parlor.

Taxpayer's Name: _____

Taxpayer's Social Security Number: _____

Tax Year: _____

Date	Activity	Name of Establishment	Accompanied by	Race Number	Amount Wagered	Amount Won	Amount Lost
	Horse and Dog Racing						

Supplemental information could include unredeemed tickets, payment records from the racetrack, and racing programs from the date of the activity.

Taxpayer's Name: _____

Taxpayer's Social Security Number: _____

Tax Year: _____

Date	Activity	Name of Lottery	Tickets Purchased	Amount Won	Amount Lost
	Lottery				

Supplemental information could include unredeemed tickets, payment slips, and winnings statements.

7

◆

Forms to the Gambler

The following two forms are very important to the gambler. Form W-2G is used to report certain gambling winnings. The form is prepared by the payer of the gambling winnings (the casino, racetrack, etc.) and a copy is provided to both the winner and the IRS.

Form 5754 is a statement made by the person(s) receiving gambling winnings if the winnings are for someone else or if a group of winners are involved. The information on the form is used by the payer to prepare the required W-2G(s)

FORM W-2G

3232	□ CORRECTED			OMB No. 1545-0238
PAYER'S name		1 Gross winnings	2 Federal income tax withheld	**2002**
Street address		3 Type of wager	4 Date won	Form W-2G
City, state, and ZIP code		5 Transaction	6 Race	Certain
Federal identification number	Telephone number	7 Winnings from identical wagers	8 Cashier	Gambling Winnings
WINNER'S name		9 Winner's taxpayer identification no.	10 Window	For Privacy Act and Paperwork Reduction Act
Street address (including apt. no.)		11 First I.D.	12 Second I.D.	Notice, see the **2002** General Instructions for Forms 1099, 1098, 5498,
City, state, and ZIP code		13 State/Payer's state identification no.	14 State income tax withheld	and W-2G. File with Form 1096.
Under penalties of perjury, I declare that, to the best of my knowledge and belief, the name, address, and taxpayer identification number that I have furnished correctly identify me as the recipient of this payment and any payments from identical wagers, and that no other person is entitled to any part of these payments.				Copy A For Internal Revenue Service Center
Signature ▶			Date ▶	
Form W-2G		Cat. No. 10138V	Department of the Treasury - Internal Revenue Service	

The payer (the casino, racetrack, etc.) must furnish a Form W-2G to you if you receive:

1. $600 or more in gambling winnings and the payout is at least 300 times the amount of the wager (except winnings from bingo, slot machines, and keno);
2. $1,200 or more in gambling winnings from bingo or slot machines,
3. $1,500 or more in proceeds (the amount of winnings less the amount of the wager) from keno; or
4. any gambling winnings subject to federal income tax withholdings.

Any federal income tax withheld on these winnings is shown in Box 2. The current federal tax-withholding rate is 28 percent on certain winnings less the wager. If you do not provide your social security number to the payer, the amount in this box may be backup withheld at a 31 percent rate.

You must sign the form if you are the only person entitled to the winnings and the winnings are subject to the regular gambling withholdings. If another person is entitled to any part of the winnings, see Form 5754.

You will receive your copies from the payer by February 2 of the year following the win. Review the form as soon as it is received and notify the payer of any errors.

FORM 5754

Form **5754** (Rev. July 2000) Department of the Treasury Internal Revenue Service	**Statement by Person(s) Receiving Gambling Winnings** ► Recipients of gambling winnings should see the instructions on the back of this form. ► Payers of gambling winnings should see the separate Instructions for Forms W-2G and 5754.			OMB No. 1545-0239 Return to payer. Do not send to the IRS.
Date won	Type of winnings	Game number	Machine number	Race number

Part I   Person to Whom Winnings Are Paid

Name		Address		
Taxpayer identification number	Other I.D.		Amount received	Federal income tax withheld

Part II   Persons to Whom Winnings Are Taxable *(continued on page 2)*

(a) Name	(b) Taxpayer identification number	(c) Address	(d) Amount won	(e) Winnings from identical wagers

Under penalties of perjury, I declare that, to the best of my knowledge and belief, the names, addresses, and taxpayer identification numbers that I have furnished correctly identify me as the recipient of this payment and correctly identify each person entitled to any part of this payment and any payments from identical wagers.

Signature ►   Date ►

For Privacy Act and Paperwork Reduction Act Notice, see back of form.   Cat. No. 12100R   Form **5754** (Rev. 7-2000)

Purpose of the Form

You must complete Form 5754 if you receive gambling winnings either for someone else or as a member of a group of winners on the same winning ticket. The information provided on the form enables the payer of the winnings to prepare Form W-2G for each winner listed and to show the taxable winnings for those individuals.

Part I

If you are the person to whom gambling winnings are paid, enter your name, address, and taxpayer identification number in Part I. If winnings are from state-conducted lotteries, the box labeled "other ID" can be left blank. The total amount received and the total federal income tax withheld must be entered in the remaining columns.

Part II

Complete Part II to identify each winner and each winner's share of the winnings. If you are also one of the winners, enter your information in Part II by entering "same as above" in columns (a), (b), and (c) and the applicable amounts in columns (d) and (e). Then complete columns (a) through (e) for each of the winners. Return the form to the payer.

The taxpayer identification number for an individual is the social security number; for all others, it is the employer identification number.

If federal income tax is withheld, the person who received the winnings must sign and date the form. If no federal income tax is withheld, no signature is required.

8

◆

Reporting Your Gambling Winnings and Losses

Gambling winnings are reported on the line for "other income" on Form 1040. Since other items are also reported on this line, you must insert the word "gambling" in the space provided (see the example in this chapter).

Gambling losses are reported on Schedule A–Itemized Deductions, in the section designated "Other Itemized Deductions." The words "gambling losses" must be inserted in the space provided (see example in this chapter).

Form 1040 Department of the Treasury—Internal Revenue Service
U.S. Individual Income Tax Return **2002** (99) IRS Use Only—Do not write or staple in this space.

For the year Jan. 1–Dec. 31, 2002, or other tax year beginning , 2002, ending , 20   OMB No. 1545-0074

Label
(See instructions on page 21.)
Use the IRS label. Otherwise, please print or type.

L A B E L   H E R E

Your first name and initial	Last name
If a joint return, spouse's first name and initial	Last name
Home address (number and street). If you have a P.O. box, see page 21.	Apt. no.
City, town or post office, state, and ZIP code. If you have a foreign address, see page 21.	

Your social security number

Spouse's social security number

▲ **Important!** ▲
You **must** enter your SSN(s) above.

Presidential Election Campaign
(See page 21.)

Note. Checking "Yes" will not change your tax or reduce your refund.
Do you, or your spouse if filing a joint return, want $3 to go to this fund? ▶

	You		Spouse	
	☐Yes	☐No	☐Yes	☐No

Filing Status
Check only one box.

1 ☐ Single
2 ☐ Married filing jointly (even if only one had income)
3 ☐ Married filing separately. Enter spouse's SSN above and full name here. ▶
4 ☐ Head of household (with qualifying person). (See page 21.) If the qualifying person is a child but not your dependent, enter this child's name here. ▶
5 ☐ Qualifying widow(er) with dependent child (year spouse died ▶). (See page 21.)

Exemptions

6a ☐ **Yourself.** If your parent (or someone else) can claim you as a dependent on his or her tax return, **do not** check box 6a
b ☐ **Spouse**

c **Dependents:**

If more than five dependents, see page 22.

(1) First name Last name	(2) Dependent's social security number	(3) Dependent's relationship to you	(4)✔ if qualifying child for child tax credit (see page 22)
			☐
			☐
			☐
			☐
			☐

No. of boxes checked on 6a and 6b ___
No. of children on 6c who:
• lived with you ___
• did not live with you due to divorce or separation (see page 22) ___
Dependents on 6c not entered above ___
Add numbers on lines above ▶ ___

d Total number of exemptions claimed

Income

Attach Forms W-2 and W-2G here. Also attach Form(s) 1099-R if tax was withheld.

If you did not get a W-2, see page 23.

Enclose, but do not attach, any payment. Also, please use Form 1040-V.

7	Wages, salaries, tips, etc. Attach Form(s) W-2	7	
8a	Taxable interest. Attach Schedule B if required	8a	
b	Tax-exempt interest. Do not include on line 8a . . .	8b	
9	Ordinary dividends. Attach Schedule B if required	9	
10	Taxable refunds, credits, or offsets of state and local income taxes (see page 24)	10	
11	Alimony received	11	
12	Business income or (loss). Attach Schedule C or C-EZ	12	
13	Capital gain or (loss). Attach Schedule D if required. If not required, check here ▶ ☐	13	
14	Other gains or (losses). Attach Form 4797	14	
15a	IRA distributions 15a	b Taxable amount (see page 25)	15b	
16a	Pensions and annuities 16a	b Taxable amount (see page 25)	16b	
17	Rental real estate, royalties, partnerships, S corporations, trusts, etc. Attach Schedule E	17	
18	Farm income or (loss). Attach Schedule F	18	
19	Unemployment compensation	19	
20a	Social security benefits 20a	b Taxable amount (see page 27)	20b	
21	Other income. List type and amount (see page 29) .Gambling Winnings..	21	
22	Add the amounts in the far right column for lines 7 through 21. This is your **total income** ▶	22	

Adjusted Gross Income

23	Educator expenses (see page 29)	23	
24	IRA deduction (see page 29)	24	
25	Student loan interest deduction (see page 31)	25	
26	Tuition and fees deduction (see page 32)	26	
27	Archer MSA deduction. Attach Form 8853	27	
28	Moving expenses. Attach Form 3903	28	
29	One-half of self-employment tax. Attach Schedule SE	29	
30	Self-employed health insurance deduction (see page 33)	30	
31	Self-employed SEP, SIMPLE, and qualified plans	31	
32	Penalty on early withdrawal of savings	32	
33a	Alimony paid b Recipient's SSN ▶	33a	
34	Add lines 23 through 33a		34	
35	Subtract line 34 from line 22. This is your **adjusted gross income** ▶		35	

For Disclosure, Privacy Act, and Paperwork Reduction Act Notice, see page 76.   Cat. No. 11320B   Form **1040** (2002)

Form 1040 (2002)   Page **2**

Tax and Credits	**36**	Amount from line 35 (adjusted gross income)	**36**
	37a	Check if: ☐ **You** were 65 or older, ☐ Blind; ☐ **Spouse** was 65 or older, ☐ Blind.	
Standard Deduction for—		Add the number of boxes checked above and enter the total here . . . . ▶ **37a** ☐	
	b	If you are married filing separately and your spouse itemizes deductions, or you were a dual-status alien, see page 34 and check here . . . . . . ▶ **37b** ☐	
• People who checked any box on line 37a or 37b or who can be claimed as a dependent, see page 34.	**38**	**Itemized deductions** (from Schedule A) **or your standard deduction** (see left margin) . .	**38**
	39	Subtract line 38 from line 36	**39**
	40	If line 36 is $103,000 or less, multiply $3,000 by the total number of exemptions claimed on line 6d. If line 36 is over $103,000, see the worksheet on page 35	**40**
• All others:	**41**	**Taxable income.** Subtract line 40 from line 39. If line 40 is more than line 39, enter -0- .	**41**
Single, $4,700	**42**	**Tax** (see page 36). Check if any tax is from: a ☐ Form(s) 8814 b ☐ Form 4972	**42**
Head of household, $6,900	**43**	**Alternative minimum tax** (see page 37). Attach Form 6251	**43**
Married filing jointly or Qualifying widow(er), $7,850	**44**	Add lines 42 and 43 . . . . ▶	**44**
	45	Foreign tax credit. Attach Form 1116 if required **45**	
	46	Credit for child and dependent care expenses. Attach Form 2441 **46**	
	47	Credit for the elderly or the disabled. Attach Schedule R . . **47**	
Married filing separately, $3,925	**48**	Education credits. Attach Form 8863 . . . . . . **48**	
	49	Retirement savings contributions credit. Attach Form 8880 . **49**	
	50	Child tax credit (see page 39) **50**	
	51	Adoption credit. Attach Form 8839 . . . . **51**	
	52	Credits from: a ☐ Form 8396 b ☐ Form 8859 . . . **52**	
	53	Other credits. Check applicable box(es): a ☐ Form 3800	
		b ☐ Form 8801 c ☐ Specify _____ **53**	
	54	Add lines 45 through 53. These are your **total credits**	**54**
	55	Subtract line 54 from line 44. If line 54 is more than line 44, enter -0-. . . . . ▶	**55**
Other Taxes	**56**	Self-employment tax. Attach Schedule SE	**56**
	57	Social security and Medicare tax on tip income not reported to employer. Attach Form 4137 .	**57**
	58	Tax on qualified plans, including IRAs, and other tax-favored accounts. Attach Form 5329 if required .	**58**
	59	Advance earned income credit payments from Form(s) W-2	**59**
	60	Household employment taxes. Attach Schedule H	**60**
	61	Add lines 55 through 60. This is your **total tax** . . . . ▶	**61**
Payments	**62**	Federal income tax withheld from Forms W-2 and 1099 . . **62**	
	63	2002 estimated tax payments and amount applied from 2001 return **63**	
If you have a qualifying child, attach Schedule EIC.	**64**	Earned income credit (EIC) **64**	
	65	Excess social security and tier 1 RRTA tax withheld (see page 56) **65**	
	66	Additional child tax credit. Attach Form 8812 . . . . **66**	
	67	Amount paid with request for extension to file (see page 56) **67**	
	68	Other payments from: a ☐ Form 2439 b ☐ Form 4136 c ☐ Form 8885 **68**	
	69	Add lines 62 through 68. These are your **total payments** . . . . ▶	**69**
Refund	**70**	If line 69 is more than line 61, subtract line 61 from line 69. This is the amount you **overpaid**	**70**
Direct deposit? See page 56 and fill in 71b, 71c, and 71d.	**71a**	Amount of line 70 you want **refunded to you** . . . . ▶	**71a**
	▶ **b**	Routing number |_|_|_|_|_|_|_|_|_| ▶ c Type: ☐ Checking ☐ Savings	
	▶ **d**	Account number |_|_|_|_|_|_|_|_|_|_|_|_|_|_|_|_|_|	
	72	Amount of line 70 you want applied to your 2003 estimated tax ▶ **72**	
Amount You Owe	**73**	**Amount you owe.** Subtract line 69 from line 61. For details on how to pay, see page 57 ▶	**73**
	74	Estimated tax penalty (see page 57) **74**	
Third Party Designee		Do you want to allow another person to discuss this return with the IRS (see page 58)? ☐ **Yes.** Complete the following. ☐ **No**
		Designee's name ▶ ____ Phone no. ▶ ( ) Personal identification number (PIN) ▶ |_|_|_|_|_|
Sign Here		Under penalties of perjury, I declare that I have examined this return and accompanying schedules and statements, and to the best of my knowledge and belief, they are true, correct, and complete. Declaration of preparer (other than taxpayer) is based on all information of which preparer has any knowledge.
Joint return? See page 21.		Your signature ____ Date ____ Your occupation ____ Daytime phone number ( )
Keep a copy for your records.	▶	Spouse's signature. If a joint return, **both must sign.** Date ____ Spouse's occupation ____
Paid Preparer's Use Only		Preparer's signature ____ Date ____ Check if self-employed ☐ Preparer's SSN or PTIN
		Firm's name (or yours if self-employed), address, and ZIP code ▶ ____ EIN ____ Phone no. ( )

Form **1040** (2002)

SCHEDULES A&B (Form 1040) Department of the Treasury Internal Revenue Service (99) Name(s) shown on Form 1040	**Schedule A— Itemized Deductions** (Schedule B is on back) ► **Attach to Form 1040.** ► **See Instructions for Schedules A and B (Form 1040).**	OMB No. 1545-0074 20**02** Attachment Sequence No. 07 Your social security number

Medical and Dental Expenses		**Caution.** Do not include expenses reimbursed or paid by others.		
	1	Medical and dental expenses (see page A-2) . . .	1	
	2	Enter amount from Form 1040, line 36 ⌊ 2		
	3	Multiply line 2 by 7.5% (.075)	3	
	4	Subtract line 3 from line 1. If line 3 is more than line 1, enter -0-		4
Taxes You Paid (See page A-2.)	5	State and local income taxes	5	
	6	Real estate taxes (see page A-2)	6	
	7	Personal property taxes	7	
	8	Other taxes. List type and amount ►	8	
	9	Add lines 5 through 8		9
Interest You Paid (See page A-3.) **Note.** Personal interest is not deductible.	10	Home mortgage interest and points reported to you on Form 1098	10	
	11	Home mortgage interest not reported to you on Form 1098. If paid to the person from whom you bought the home, see page A-3 and show that person's name, identifying no., and address ►	11	
	12	Points not reported to you on Form 1098. See page A-3 for special rules	12	
	13	Investment interest. Attach Form 4952 if required. (See page A-3.)	13	
	14	Add lines 10 through 13		14
Gifts to Charity If you made a gift and got a benefit for it, see page A-4.	15	Gifts by cash or check. If you made any gift of $250 or more, see page A-4	15	
	16	Other than by cash or check. If any gift of $250 or more, see page A-4. You **must** attach Form 8283 if over $500	16	
	17	Carryover from prior year	17	
	18	Add lines 15 through 17		18
Casualty and Theft Losses	19	Casualty or theft loss(es). Attach Form 4684. (See page A-5.)		19
Job Expenses and Most Other Miscellaneous Deductions (See page A-5 for expenses to deduct here.)	20	Unreimbursed employee expenses—job travel, union dues, job education, etc. You **must** attach Form 2106 or 2106-EZ if required. (See page A-5.) ►	20	
	21	Tax preparation fees	21	
	22	Other expenses—investment, safe deposit box, etc. List type and amount ►	22	
	23	Add lines 20 through 22	23	
	24	Enter amount from Form 1040, line 36 ⌊ 24 ⌊		
	25	Multiply line 24 by 2% (.02)	25	
	26	Subtract line 25 from line 23. If line 25 is more than line 23, enter -0-		26
Other Miscellaneous Deductions	27	Other—from list on page A-6. List type and amount ► .... Gambling Losses		
Total Itemized Deductions	28	Is Form 1040, line 36, over $137,300 (over $68,650 if married filing separately ☐ **No.** Your deduction is not limited. Add the amounts in the far right column for lines 4 through 27. Also, enter this amount on Form 1040, line 38. ► ☐ **Yes.** Your deduction may be limited. See page A-6 for the amount to enter.		

For Paperwork Reduction Act Notice, see Form 1040 instructions.   Cat. No. 11330X   Schedule A (Form 1040) 2002

9

$\blacklozenge$

Cohan Rule

USE OF ESTIMATES

The general rule, when dealing with the IRS, requires taxpayers to substantiate all deductions. The burden of proof falls on the taxpayer. Under certain circumstances, a court may waive this requirement and allow the use of estimates. The U.S. Court of Appeals for the Second Circuit in the case of G. M. Cohan established that under certain circumstances, estimates may be used. This rule (known as the Cohan Rule) applies when the taxpayer is unquestionably entitled to a deduction, but the amount is not adequately substantiated. For this rule to apply, the taxpayer must convince the court that:

- Expenses were incurred
- There is something upon which the estimates can be based. In some cases, the court will use its own experience in estimating expenses.

THE TAXPAYER

John David Zielonka identified himself on his tax returns as a professional gambler. During the years 1989 and 1992, the years in question, Zielonka attended the dog and horse tracks on a regular and frequent basis. During those years, the taxpayer gambled on a full-time basis and was not gainfully employed.

For the years 1989 and 1992, Zielonka did not present any books or records to show his gambling winnings or losses. He did not remember if he kept any books for 1989. He did maintain a gambling diary for 1992. However, in his opinion, it was probably not accurate because it was "too time consuming to . . . make it precise."

On his 1989 tax return he reported winnings of $29,978, and in 1992 he reported $140,830 in winnings. The 1989 amount matched the total amount reported to him on Form W-2G by the gambling establishment. The 1992 amount represented $90,830 reported to him on Form W-2G and $50,000 of additional estimated winnings. On Schedule A, the taxpayer deducted estimated gambling losses of $29,978 for 1989 and $140,830 for 1992.

THE IRS

The IRS audited Zielonka's 1989 and 1992 tax returns. Due to a lack of substantiation, the IRS disallowed the gambling losses and assessed a tax deficiency for each year.

THE COURT AND THE DECISION

The Court ruled in favor of the IRS. The Court addressed the fact that:

- The taxpayer would be entitled to a deduction for losses from gambling transactions to the extent of gains from such transactions. However, these losses must be substantiated.
- The taxpayer bears the burden of proving the IRS has erred in disallowing the deduction for the gambling losses.
- The taxpayer is required to keep books and records to substantiate income and deductions.
- If the record provides sufficient evidence that the taxpayer has incurred deductible expenses, but the taxpayer is not able to

substantiate the exact amount, the Court may, under certain circumstances, allow the use of an estimate. However, there must be some basis upon which the estimate may be made.

The Court recognized that the taxpayer must have some losses. However, consideration was also given to the fact that the taxpayer only reported winnings in 1989 that were reported to him on Form W-2G. Thus, the Court did not feel comfortable that all winnings were reported. This uncertainty, together with the total absence of any documentation or other corroborating evidence concerning the gambling activity, precluded the Court from considering the use of estimates under the Cohan Rule in this case.

Author's Note: The Court did not address the inconsistency of the taxpayer claiming to be a professional gambler yet listing the deductions on Schedule A rather than Schedule C. The Court, because of its holding that no deductions were allowed, did not need to address the taxpayer's situation as an amateur or professional gambler.

THE COHAN RULE

The general rule requires the taxpayer to substantiate its deductions. Under certain circumstances, a court may waive this requirement. When a taxpayer is unquestionably entitled to some deduction, but the amount is not properly substantiated, the court may make an allowance based on an estimate (G. M. Cohan). To allow the use of estimates under the Cohan Rule, the court must be convinced that:

- The expense was incurred by the taxpayer.
- There is a basis upon which to estimate the allowance.

In the case of *Doffin* v. *Commissioner*, the Tax Court applied the Cohan Rule and allowed estimated losses of approximately $64,000 after the IRS only allowed $247.

The Court also estimated the taxpayer's losses under the Cohan Rule in the case of F. M. Delgozzo.

The Court determined the Cohan Rule did not apply in the case of A. Plisco since reliable figures were not available to calculate the estimates.

Author's Comment: The Cohan Rule is not an alternative to proper record keeping. The only way to be certain the losses you claim will be accepted is through proper documentation.

10

◆

Preparing a Gambler's
Tax Return

Beware of This Hidden Tax Trap!

When preparing their taxes, gamblers too often make the mistake of assuming that a given amount of winnings will be offset, or canceled out, by an equal amount of gambling losses, and that is *not* necessarily so! The danger lies in the fact that gambling losses, like any other itemized deduction, have no effect whatsoever on your Adjusted Gross Income, which can effect many other tax calculations, including the amount of tax on your Social Security benefits, the amount you can deduct for medical expenses, and so forth (see question 10).

In the following example, you will see how this tax trap affected the return of John and Jane Taxpayer.

FACTS

John and Jane Taxpayer are both retired and are sixty-four years old. They have income from the following sources:

(1) Savings accounts and certificates of deposit—$2,500.
(2) Fully taxable dividends from a stock they own—$1,500.
(3) John is a retired corporate manager and receives a taxable pension of $26,000. Jane's taxable pension is $10,000.

(4) John and Jane's combined Social Security benefits are $16,500.

(5) John and Jane own their own home. During 2002, they paid $2,200 in real estate taxes.

(6) They also paid $300 in personal property taxes.

(7) During the year they made deductible gifts to charities in the amount of $2,400.

(8) John and Jane have a total of $5,200 withheld from their pensions for federal income taxes.

This information has been recorded and referenced on the following tax returns.

SITUATION 1

While reviewing their tax return, they noticed the standard deduction amount (Form 1040, Line 38) was larger than their itemized deduction amount (Schedule A, Line 28). Therefore, they were entitled to deduct the larger standard deduction amount. They also noticed they were receiving a refund of $436, which was what they were accustomed to. John and Jane's tax return is presented on the following pages.

SITUATION 1

Form **1040**	Department of the Treasury—Internal Revenue Service **U.S. Individual Income Tax Return** **2002**	(99) IRS Use Only—Do not write or staple in this space.

For the year Jan. 1–Dec. 31, 2002, or other tax year beginning _____ , 2002, ending _____ , 20 ____

OMB No. 1545-0074

Label
(See instructions on page 21.)
Use the IRS label. Otherwise, please print or type.

L A B E L   H E R E

Your first name and initial: **John**   Last name: **Taxpayer**
Your social security number: **001 : 01 : 0001**

If a joint return, spouse's first name and initial: **Jane**   Last name: **Taxpayer**
Spouse's social security number: **002 : 02 : 0002**

Home address (number and street). If you have a P.O. box, see page 21.   Apt. no.: **123 Any Street**

City, town or post office, state, and ZIP code. If you have a foreign address, see page 21.: **Anywhere   PA   10001**

▲ **Important!** ▲
You must enter your SSN(s) above.

Presidential Election Campaign
(See page 21.)
Note. Checking "Yes" will not change your tax or reduce your refund.
Do you, or your spouse if filing a joint return, want $3 to go to this fund? . . . . ►
You: ☒Yes ☐No   Spouse: ☒Yes ☐No

Filing Status
Check only one box.

1 ☐ Single
2 ☒ Married filing jointly (even if only one had income)
3 ☐ Married filing separately. Enter spouse's SSN above and full name here. ►
4 ☐ Head of household (with qualifying person). (See page 21.) If the qualifying person is a child but not your dependent, enter this child's name here. ►
5 ☐ Qualifying widow(er) with dependent child (year spouse died ►). (See page 21.)

Exemptions

6a ☐ Yourself. If your parent (or someone else) can claim you as a dependent on his or her tax return, do not check box 6a . . . .
b ☐ Spouse . . . .
c Dependents:

(1) First name Last name	(2) Dependent's social security number	(3) Dependent's relationship to you	(4) ✓ if qualifying child for child tax credit (see page 22)
			☐
			☐
			☐
			☐
			☐

If more than five dependents, see page 22.

No. of boxes checked on 6a and 6b ____
No. of children on 6c who:
• lived with you ____
• did not live with you due to divorce or separation (see page 22) ____
Dependents on 6c not entered above ____
Add numbers on lines above ► ☐

d   Total number of exemptions claimed . . . .

Income

Attach Forms W-2 and W-2G here. Also attach Form(s) 1099-R if tax was withheld.

If you did not get a W-2, see page 23.

Enclose, but do not attach, any payment. Also, please use Form 1040-V.

7	Wages, salaries, tips, etc. Attach Form(s) W-2	**7**
8a	Taxable interest. Attach Schedule B if required	**8a** 2,500 (1)
b	Tax-exempt interest. Do not include on line 8a . . . 8b	
9	Ordinary dividends. Attach Schedule B if required	**9** 1,500 (2)
10	Taxable refunds, credits, or offsets of state and local income taxes (see page 24) . .	**10**
11	Alimony received	**11**
12	Business income or (loss). Attach Schedule C or C-EZ	**12**
13	Capital gain or (loss). Attach Schedule D if required. If not required, check here ► ☐	**13**
14	Other gains or (losses). Attach Form 4797	**14**
15a	IRA distributions . . 15a	b Taxable amount (see page 25)	**15b**
16a	Pensions and annuities 16a	b Taxable amount (see page 25)	**16b** 36,000 (3)
17	Rental real estate, royalties, partnerships, S corporations, trusts, etc. Attach Schedule E	**17**
18	Farm income or (loss). Attach Schedule F	**18**
19	Unemployment compensation	**19**
20a	Social security benefits 20a 16,500 (4)	b Taxable amount (see page 27)	**20b** 9,613
21	Other income. List type and amount (see page 29)	**21**
22	Add the amounts in the far right column for lines 7 through 21. This is your **total income** ►	**22** 49,613

Adjusted Gross Income

23	Educator expenses (see page 29)	23
24	IRA deduction (see page 29)	24
25	Student loan interest deduction (see page 31) . . .	25
26	Tuition and fees deduction (see page 32)	26
27	Archer MSA deduction. Attach Form 8853	27
28	Moving expenses. Attach Form 3903	28
29	One-half of self-employment tax. Attach Schedule SE .	29
30	Self-employed health insurance deduction (see page 33)	30
31	Self-employed SEP, SIMPLE, and qualified plans . .	31
32	Penalty on early withdrawal of savings	32
33a	Alimony paid b Recipient's SSN ►	33a
34	Add lines 23 through 33a . . . . ►	34
35	Subtract line 34 from line 22. This is your **adjusted gross income** . . . . ►	**35** 49,613

For Disclosure, Privacy Act, and Paperwork Reduction Act Notice, see page 76.   Cat. No. 11320B   Form **1040** (2002)

SITUATION 1

Form 1040 (2002) ~   Page 2

Tax and Credits	36	Amount from line 35 (adjusted gross income)	36	49,613
Standard Deduction for—	37a	Check if: ☐ You were 65 or older, ☐ Blind; ☐ Spouse was 65 or older, ☐ Blind. Add the number of boxes checked above and enter the total here . . . . ▶ 37a		
• People who checked any box on line 37a or 37b or who can be claimed as a dependent, see page 34.	b	If you are married filing separately and your spouse itemizes deductions, or you were a dual-status alien, see page 34 and check here . . . . . . ▶ 37b ☐		
	38	Itemized deductions (from Schedule A) or your standard deduction (see left margin) . .	38	7,850
	39	Subtract line 38 from line 36	39	41,763
	40	If line 36 is $103,000 or less, multiply $3,000 by the total number of exemptions claimed on line 6d. If line 36 is over $103,000, see the worksheet on page 35	40	6,000
• All others: Single, $4,700	41	Taxable income. Subtract line 40 from line 39. If line 40 is more than line 39, enter -0- .	41	35,763
Head of household, $6,900	42	Tax (see page 36). Check if any tax is from: a ☐ Form(s) 8814 b ☐ Form 4972 . . .	42	4,764
Married filing jointly or Qualifying widow(er), $7,850	43	Alternative minimum tax (see page 37). Attach Form 6251	43	
	44	Add lines 42 and 43 . . . . ▶	44	4,764
Married filing separately, $3,925	45	Foreign tax credit. Attach Form 1116 if required	45	
	46	Credit for child and dependent care expenses. Attach Form 2441	46	
	47	Credit for the elderly or the disabled. Attach Schedule R . .	47	
	48	Education credits. Attach Form 8863	48	
	49	Retirement savings contributions credit. Attach Form 8880 . .	49	
	50	Child tax credit (see page 39)	50	
	51	Adoption credit. Attach Form 8839	51	
	52	Credits from: a ☐ Form 8396 b ☐ Form 8859 . . .	52	
	53	Other credits. Check applicable box(es): a ☐ Form 3800 b ☐ Form 8801 c ☐ Specify _____	53	
	54	Add lines 45 through 53. These are your total credits	54	
	55	Subtract line 54 from line 44. If line 54 is more than line 44, enter -0- . . . . . ▶	55	4,764
Other Taxes	56	Self-employment tax. Attach Schedule SE	56	
	57	Social security and Medicare tax on tip income not reported to employer. Attach Form 4137 .	57	
	58	Tax on qualified plans, including IRAs, and other tax-favored accounts. Attach Form 5329 if required .	58	
	59	Advance earned income credit payments from Form(s) W-2 . .	59	
	60	Household employment taxes. Attach Schedule H	60	
	61	Add lines 55 through 60. This is your total tax . . . . ▶	61	4,764
Payments	62	Federal income tax withheld from Forms W-2 and 1099 . .	62	5,200 (8)
If you have a qualifying child, attach Schedule EIC.	63	2002 estimated tax payments and amount applied from 2001 return	63	
	64	Earned income credit (EIC)	64	
	65	Excess social security and tier 1 RRTA tax withheld (see page 56)	65	
	66	Additional child tax credit. Attach Form 8812	66	
	67	Amount paid with request for extension to file (see page 56)	67	
	68	Other payments from: a ☐ Form 2439 b ☐ Form 4136 c ☐ Form 8885	68	
	69	Add lines 62 through 68. These are your total payments . . . . ▶	69	5,200
Refund	70	If line 69 is more than line 61, subtract line 61 from line 69. This is the amount you overpaid ▶	70	436
Direct deposit? See page 56 and fill in 71b, 71c, and 71d.	71a	Amount of line 70 you want refunded to you . . . . ▶	71a	436
	▶ b	Routing number [_____] ▶ c Type: ☐ Checking ☐ Savings		
	▶ d	Account number [_____]		
	72	Amount of line 70 you want applied to your 2003 estimated tax ▶	72	
Amount You Owe	73	Amount you owe. Subtract line 69 from line 61. For details on how to pay, see page 57 ▶	73	
	74	Estimated tax penalty (see page 57)	74	

Third Party Designee	Do you want to allow another person to discuss this return with the IRS (see page 58)? ☐ Yes. Complete the following. ☐ No
	Designee's name ▶ Phone no. ▶ ( ) Personal identification number (PIN) ▶ [_____]
Sign Here	Under penalties of perjury, I declare that I have examined this return and accompanying schedules and statements, and to the best of my knowledge and belief, they are true, correct, and complete. Declaration of preparer (other than taxpayer) is based on all information of which preparer has any knowledge.
Joint return? See page 21. Keep a copy for your records.	Your signature Date Your occupation: Retired Daytime phone number ( )
	Spouse's signature. If a joint return, both must sign. Date Spouse's occupation: Retired
Paid Preparer's Use Only	Preparer's signature Date Check if self-employed ☐ Preparer's SSN or PTIN
	Firm's name (or yours if self-employed), address, and ZIP code ▶ EIN Phone no. ( )

Form **1040** (2002)

SITUATION 1

SCHEDULES A&B (Form 1040)	Schedule A— Itemized Deductions (Schedule B is on back)	OMB No. 1545-0074 2002 Attachment Sequence No. 07
Department of the Treasury Internal Revenue Service (99)	▶ Attach to Form 1040. ▶ See Instructions for Schedules A and B (Form 1040).	
Name(s) shown on Form 1040		Your social security number

Medical and Dental Expenses		Caution. Do not include expenses reimbursed or paid by others.			
	1	Medical and dental expenses (see page A-2) . . .	1		
	2	Enter amount from Form 1040, line 36 [2]			
	3	Multiply line 2 by 7.5% (.075)	3		
	4	Subtract line 3 from line 1. If line 3 is more than line 1, enter -0-		4	
Taxes You Paid (See page A-2.)	5	State and local income taxes	5		
	6	Real estate taxes (see page A-2)	6	2,200 (5)	
	7	Personal property taxes	7	300 (6)	
	8	Other taxes. List type and amount ▶	8		
	9	Add lines 5 through 8		9	2,500
Interest You Paid (See page A-3.)	10	Home mortgage interest and points reported to you on Form 1098	10		
	11	Home mortgage interest not reported to you on Form 1098. If paid to the person from whom you bought the home, see page A-3 and show that person's name, identifying no., and address ▶	11		
Note. Personal interest is not deductible.	12	Points not reported to you on Form 1098. See page A-3 for special rules	12		
	13	Investment interest. Attach Form 4952 if required. (See page A-3.)	13		
	14	Add lines 10 through 13		14	
Gifts to Charity If you made a gift and got a benefit for it, see page A-4.	15	Gifts by cash or check. If you made any gift of $250 or more, see page A-4	15	2,400 (7)	
	16	Other than by cash or check. If any gift of $250 or more, see page A-4. You must attach Form 8283 if over $500	16		
	17	Carryover from prior year	17		
	18	Add lines 15 through 17		18	2,400
Casualty and Theft Losses	19	Casualty or theft loss(es). Attach Form 4684. (See page A-5.)		19	
Job Expenses and Most Other Miscellaneous Deductions (See page A-5 for expenses to deduct here.)	20	Unreimbursed employee expenses—job travel, union dues, job education, etc. You must attach Form 2106 or 2106-EZ if required. (See page A-5.) ▶	20		
	21	Tax preparation fees	21		
	22	Other expenses—investment, safe deposit box, etc. List type and amount ▶	22		
	23	Add lines 20 through 22	23		
	24	Enter amount from Form 1040, line 36 [24]			
	25	Multiply line 24 by 2% (.02)	25		
	26	Subtract line 25 from line 23. If line 25 is more than line 23, enter -0-		26	
Other Miscellaneous Deductions	27	Other—from list on page A-6. List type and amount ▶		27	
Total Itemized Deductions	28	Is Form 1040, line 36, over $137,300 (over $68,650 if married filing separately)? ☐ No. Your deduction is not limited. Add the amounts in the far right column for lines 4 through 27. Also, enter this amount on Form 1040, line 38. ☐ Yes. Your deduction may be limited. See page A-6 for the amount to enter.	▶	28	4,900

For Paperwork Reduction Act Notice, see Form 1040 Instructions.   Cat. No. 11330X   Schedule A (Form 1040) 2002

SITUATION 1

Name(s) shown on Form 1040. Do not enter name and social security number if shown on other side.   OMB No. 1545-0074   Page **2**

Your social security number

Schedule B—Interest and Ordinary Dividends

Attachment Sequence No. **08**

			Amount	
Part I **Interest** (See page B-1 and the instructions for Form 1040, line 8a.)	**1** List name of payer. If any interest is from a seller-financed mortgage and the buyer used the property as a personal residence, see page B-1 and list this interest first. Also, show that buyer's social security number and address ▶			
	Local Bank and Trust		800	
	Local Savings and Loan		1,300	
	Local Credit Union		400	
		1		
Note. If you received a Form 1099-INT, Form 1099-OID, or substitute statement from a brokerage firm, list the firm's name as the payer and enter the total interest shown on that form.				
	2 Add the amounts on line 1	**2**	2,500	
	3 Excludable interest on series EE and I U.S. savings bonds issued after 1989 from Form 8815, line 14. You **must** attach Form 8815	**3**		
	4 Subtract line 3 from line 2. Enter the result here and on Form 1040, line 8a ▶	**4**	2,500	(1)
	Note. If line 4 is over $1,500, you must complete Part III.			
			Amount	
Part II **Ordinary Dividends** (See page B-1 and the instructions for Form 1040, line 9.)	**5** List name of payer. Include only ordinary dividends. If you received any capital gain distributions, see the instructions for Form 1040, line 13 ▶			
	Any Corporation		1,500	
Note. If you received a Form 1099-DIV or substitute statement from a brokerage firm, list the firm's name as the payer and enter the ordinary dividends shown on that form.		**5**		
	6 Add the amounts on line 5. Enter the total here and on Form 1040, line 9 ▶	**6**	1,500	(2)
	Note. If line 6 is over $1,500, you must complete Part III.			

		Yes	No
Part III **Foreign Accounts and Trusts** (See page B-2.)	You must complete this part if you **(a)** had over $1,500 of taxable interest or ordinary dividends; OR **(b)** had a foreign account; or **(c)** received a distribution from, or were a grantor of, or a transferor to, a foreign trust.		
	7a At any time during 2002, did you have an interest in or a signature or other authority over a financial account in a foreign country, such as a bank account, securities account, or other financial account? See page B-2 for exceptions and filing requirements for Form TD F 90-22.1		
	b If "Yes," enter the name of the foreign country ▶		
	8 During 2002, did you receive a distribution from, or were you the grantor of, or transferor to, a foreign trust? If "Yes," you may have to file Form 3520. See page B-2		

For Paperwork Reduction Act Notice, see Form 1040 instructions.   Schedule B (Form 1040) 2002

SITUATION 1

Social Security Benefits Worksheet—Lines 20a and 20b   *Keep for Your Records*

Before you begin:
✓ Complete Form 1040, lines 21, 23, and 25 through 31a, if they apply to you.
✓ Figure any amount to be entered on the dotted line next to line 32 (see page 30).
✓ If you are married filing separately and you **lived apart** from your spouse for all of 2001, enter "D" to the right of the word "benefits" on line 20a.
✓ Be sure you have read the **Exception** on page 25 to see if you can use this worksheet instead of a publication to find out if any of your benefits are taxable.

1. Enter the total amount from **box 5** of all your **Forms SSA-1099** and
   RRB-1099 . . . . 1. ___16,500___
2. Is the amount on line 1 more than zero?

   ☐ **No.** (STOP) None of your social security benefits are taxable.

   ☐ **Yes.** Enter one-half of line 1 . . . . 2. ___8,250___
3. Add the amounts on Form 1040, lines 7, 8a, 9 through 14, 15b, 16b, 17 through 19, and 21.
   Do not include amounts from box 5 of Forms SSA-1099 or RRB-1099 . . . . 3. ___40,000___
4. Enter the amount, if any, from Form 1040, line 8b . . . . 4. _____
5. Add lines 2, 3, and 4 . . . . 5. ___48,250___
6. Add the amounts on Form 1040, lines 23, and 25 through 31a, and any amount you entered
   on the dotted line next to line 32 . . . . 6. _____
7. Subtract line 6 from line 5. If zero or less, **stop here.** None of your social security benefits
   are taxable . . . . 7. ___48,250___
8. Enter: $25,000 if single, head of household, qualifying widow(er), or married filing separately
   and you **lived apart** from your spouse for all of 2001; $32,000 if married filing jointly; -0-
   if married filing separately and you lived with your spouse at any time in 2001. . . . . 8. ___32,000___
9. Is the amount on line 8 less than the amount on line 7?

   ☐ **No.** (STOP) None of your social security benefits are taxable. You do not have to enter any
   amounts on lines 20a or 20b of Form 1040. **But** if you are married filing
   separately and you **lived apart** from your spouse for all of 2001, enter -0- on
   line 20b. Be sure you entered "D" to the right of the word "benefits" on
   line 20a.

   ☐ **Yes.** Subtract line 8 from line 7 . . . . 9. ___16,250___
10. Enter: $9,000 if single, head of household, qualifying widow(er), or married filing separately
    and you **lived apart** from your spouse for all of 2001; $12,000 if married filing jointly; -0-
    if married filing separately and you lived with your spouse at any time in 2001. . . . . 10. ___12,000___
11. Subtract line 10 from line 9. If zero or less, enter -0- . . . . 11. ___4,250___
12. Enter the **smaller** of line 9 or line 10. . . . . 12. ___12,000___
13. Enter one-half of line 12 . . . . 13. ___6,000___
14. Enter the **smaller** of line 2 or line 13. . . . . 14. ___6,000___
15. Multiply line 11 by 85% (.85). If line 11 is zero, enter -0- . . . . 15. ___3,613___
16. Add lines 14 and 15. . . . . 16. ___9,613___
17. Multiply line 1 by 85% (.85). . . . . 17. ___14,025___
18. **Taxable social security benefits.** Enter the **smaller** of line 16 or line 17 . . . . 18. ___9,613___
   ● Enter the amount from line 1 above on Form 1040, line 20a.
   ● Enter the amount from line 18 above on Form 1040, line 20b.

(TIP)   If part of your benefits are taxable for 2001 **and** they include benefits paid in 2001 that were for an earlier
year, you may be able to reduce the taxable amount. See Pub. 915 for details.

SITUATION 2

Since they retired, they used their refund to offset some of their expenses on their annual trip to the casino. As they began to plan this year's trip, Jane remembered that she won $2,500 on last year's trip. Luckily, they had not signed and mailed their return. John thought it would be no problem to change the return since they had documented gambling losses in excess of $2,500 during the year, and knew they were permitted to offset gambling winnings with losses. After reviewing the tax filing instructions, John and Jane had determined the $2,500 gambling winnings had to be reported on Form 1040, Line 21. Their gambling losses, to the extent of their gambling winnings, had to be recorded on Schedule A–Itemized Deductions, Line 27.

They then began to recalculate their gross income.

Their first surprise was that a larger portion of their Social Security is taxable. Without the $2,500 of gambling winnings, $9,613 of the $16,500 they received is taxable. After reporting their gambling winnings, the taxable portion of their Social Security is now $11,738, an increase of $2,125.

Their next surprise was the deduction they were entitled to on Form 1040, Line 38. Since their itemized deduction amount, including the $2,500 of gambling losses, was still below the standard deduction amount, they received no benefit from the gambling losses.

The final surprise was the bottom line. Instead of receiving a refund of $436, they now owed $258.

SITUATION 2

Form **1040**	Department of the Treasury—Internal Revenue Service **U.S. Individual Income Tax Return** 20**02**	(99)	IRS Use Only—Do not write or staple in this space.

For the year Jan. 1–Dec. 31, 2002, or other tax year beginning   , 2002, ending   , 20 | OMB No. 1545-0074

Label (See instructions on page 21.) Use the IRS label. Otherwise, please print or type.

Your first name and initial: John   Last name: Taxpayer
Your social security number: 001 : 01 : 0001

If a joint return, spouse's first name and initial: Jane   Last name: Taxpayer
Spouse's social security number: 002 : 02 : 0002

Home address (number and street). If you have a P.O. box, see page 21. — 123 Any Street   Apt. no.

City, town or post office, state, and ZIP code. If you have a foreign address, see page 21. — Anywhere PA 00001

▲ **Important!** ▲ You must enter your SSN(s) above.

Presidential Election Campaign (See page 21.)
Note. Checking "Yes" will not change your tax or reduce your refund.
Do you, or your spouse if filing a joint return, want $3 to go to this fund? ►
You: ☒Yes ☐No   Spouse: ☒Yes ☐No

Filing Status — Check only one box.
1 ☐ Single
2 ☒ Married filing jointly (even if only one had income)
3 ☐ Married filing separately. Enter spouse's SSN above and full name here. ►
4 ☐ Head of household (with qualifying person). (See page 21.) If the qualifying person is a child but not your dependent, enter this child's name here. ►
5 ☐ Qualifying widow(er) with dependent child (year spouse died ►). (See page 21.)

Exemptions
6a ☐ Yourself. If your parent (or someone else) can claim you as a dependent on his or her tax return, **do not** check box 6a
b ☐ Spouse
c Dependents:
(1) First name   Last name | (2) Dependent's social security number | (3) Dependent's relationship to you | (4)✓ if qualifying child for child tax credit (see page 22)

If more than five dependents, see page 22.

No. of boxes checked on 6a and 6b ___
No. of children on 6c who:
• lived with you ___
• did not live with you due to divorce or separation (see page 22) ___
Dependents on 6c not entered above ___
Add numbers on lines above ► ___

d Total number of exemptions claimed

Income

Attach Forms W-2 and W-2G here. Also attach Form(s) 1099-R if tax was withheld.

If you did not get a W-2, see page 23.

Enclose, but do not attach, any payment. Also, please use Form 1040-V.

7	Wages, salaries, tips, etc. Attach Form(s) W-2	7	
8a	Taxable interest. Attach Schedule B if required	8a	2,500
b	Tax-exempt interest. Do not include on line 8a . 8b		
9	Ordinary dividends. Attach Schedule B if required	9	1,500
10	Taxable refunds, credits, or offsets of state and local income taxes (see page 24)	10	
11	Alimony received	11	
12	Business income or (loss). Attach Schedule C or C-EZ	12	
13	Capital gain or (loss). Attach Schedule D if required. If not required, check here ► ☐	13	
14	Other gains or (losses). Attach Form 4797	14	
15a	IRA distributions . 15a	b Taxable amount (see page 25)	15b	
16a	Pensions and annuities 16a	b Taxable amount (see page 25)	16b	36,000
17	Rental real estate, royalties, partnerships, S corporations, trusts, etc. Attach Schedule E	17	
18	Farm income or (loss). Attach Schedule F	18	
19	Unemployment compensation	19	
20a	Social security benefits . 20a	b Taxable amount (see page 27)	20b	11,738
21	Other income. List type and amount (see page 29) Gambling Winnings ►	21	2,500
22	Add the amounts in the far right column for lines 7 through 21. This is your **total income** ►	22	54,238

Adjusted Gross Income

23	Educator expenses (see page 29)	23	
24	IRA deduction (see page 29)	24	
25	Student loan interest deduction (see page 31)	25	
26	Tuition and fees deduction (see page 32)	26	
27	Archer MSA deduction. Attach Form 8853	27	
28	Moving expenses. Attach Form 3903	28	
29	One-half of self-employment tax. Attach Schedule SE	29	
30	Self-employed health insurance deduction (see page 33)	30	
31	Self-employed SEP, SIMPLE, and qualified plans	31	
32	Penalty on early withdrawal of savings	32	
33a	Alimony paid b Recipient's SSN ►	33a	
34	Add lines 23 through 33a	34	
35	Subtract line 34 from line 22. This is your **adjusted gross income** ►	35	54,238

For Disclosure, Privacy Act, and Paperwork Reduction Act Notice, see page 76.   Cat. No. 11320B   Form **1040** (2002)

SITUATION 2

Form 1040 (2002)   Page **2**

Tax and Credits	36	Amount from line 35 (adjusted gross income)	36	54,238
	37a	Check if: ☐ You were 65 or older, ☐ Blind; ☐ Spouse was 65 or older, ☐ Blind. Add the number of boxes checked above and the total here ► 37a		
Standard Deduction for—	b	If you are married filing separately and your spouse itemizes deductions, or you were a dual-status alien, see page 34 and check here ► 37b ☐		
• People who checked any box on line 37a or 37b or who can be claimed as a dependent, see page 34.	38	Itemized deductions (from Schedule A) or your standard deduction (see left margin)	38	7,850
	39	Subtract line 38 from line 36	39	46,388
	40	If line 36 is $103,000 or less, multiply $3,000 by the total number of exemptions claimed on line 6d. If line 36 is over $103,000, see the worksheet on page 35	40	6,000
• All others:	41	Taxable income. Subtract line 40 from line 39. If line 40 is more than line 39, enter -0-	41	40,388
Single, $4,700	42	Tax (see page 36). Check if any tax is from: a ☐ Form(s) 8814 b ☐ Form 4972	42	5,458
Head of household, $6,900	43	Alternative minimum tax (see page 37). Attach Form 6251	43	
	44	Add lines 42 and 43 ►	44	5,458
Married filing jointly or Qualifying widow(er), $7,850	45	Foreign tax credit. Attach Form 1116 if required	45	
	46	Credit for child and dependent care expenses. Attach Form 2441	46	
	47	Credit for the elderly or the disabled. Attach Schedule R	47	
Married filing separately, $3,925	48	Education credits. Attach Form 8863	48	
	49	Retirement savings contributions credit. Attach Form 8880	49	
	50	Child tax credit (see page 39)	50	
	51	Adoption credit. Attach Form 8839	51	
	52	Credits from: a ☐ Form 8396 b ☐ Form 8859	52	
	53	Other credits. Check applicable box(es): a ☐ Form 3800 b ☐ Form 8801 c ☐ Specify	53	
	54	Add lines 45 through 53. These are your total credits	54	
	55	Subtract line 54 from line 44. If line 54 is more than line 44, enter -0- ►	55	5,458
Other Taxes	56	Self-employment tax. Attach Schedule SE	56	
	57	Social security and Medicare tax on tip income not reported to employer. Attach Form 4137	57	
	58	Tax on qualified plans, including IRAs, and other tax-favored accounts. Attach Form 5329 if required	58	
	59	Advance earned income credit payments from Form(s) W-2	59	
	60	Household employment taxes. Attach Schedule H	60	
	61	Add lines 55 through 60. This is your total tax ►	61	5,458
Payments	62	Federal income tax withheld from Forms W-2 and 1099 : 62	5,200	
	63	2002 estimated tax payments and amount applied from 2001 return : 63		
If you have a qualifying child, attach Schedule EIC.	64	Earned income credit (EIC) : 64		
	65	Excess social security and tier 1 RRTA tax withheld (see page 56) : 65		
	66	Additional child tax credit. Attach Form 8812 : 66		
	67	Amount paid with request for extension to file (see page 56) : 67		
	68	Other payments from: a ☐ Form 2439 b ☐ Form 4136 c ☐ Form 8885 : 68		
	69	Add lines 62 through 68. These are your total payments ►	69	5,200
Refund	70	If line 69 is more than line 61, subtract line 61 from line 69. This is the amount you overpaid	70	
Direct deposit? See page 56 and fill in 71b, 71c, and 71d.	71a	Amount of line 70 you want refunded to you	71a	
	►b	Routing number		
	►d	Account number ► c Type: ☐ Checking ☐ Savings		
	72	Amount of line 70 you want applied to your 2003 estimated tax ► 72		
Amount You Owe	73	Amount you owe. Subtract line 69 from line 61. For details on how to pay, see page 57 ►	73	258
	74	Estimated tax penalty (see page 57) : 74		

Third Party Designee   Do you want to allow another person to discuss this return with the IRS (see page 58)? ☐ Yes. Complete the following. ☐ No

Designee's name ►   Phone no. ► ( )   Personal identification number (PIN) ►

Sign Here   Under penalties of perjury, I declare that I have examined this return and accompanying schedules and statements, and to the best of my knowledge and belief, they are true, correct, and complete. Declaration of preparer (other than taxpayer) is based on all information of which preparer has any knowledge.

Joint return? See page 21. Keep a copy for your records.

Your signature   Date   Your occupation: Retired   Daytime phone number ( )

Spouse's signature. If a joint return, both must sign.   Date   Spouse's occupation: Retired

Paid Preparer's Use Only   Preparer's signature ►   Date   Check if self-employed ☐   Preparer's SSN or PTIN

Firm's name (or yours if self-employed), address, and ZIP code ►   EIN   Phone no. ( )

Form **1040** (2002)

SITUATION 2

SCHEDULES A&B		**Schedule A— Itemized Deductions**		OMB No. 1545-0074
(Form 1040)		(Schedule B is on back)		**20**02
Department of the Treasury Internal Revenue Service (99)		▶ Attach to Form 1040. ▶ See Instructions for Schedules A and B (Form 1040).		Attachment Sequence No. 07
Name(s) shown on Form 1040				Your social security number

Medical and Dental Expenses		Caution. Do not include expenses reimbursed or paid by others.			
	1	Medical and dental expenses (see page A-2) . . .	1		
	2	Enter amount from Form 1040, line 36 [2]			
	3	Multiply line 2 by 7.5% (.075).	3		
	4	Subtract line 3 from line 1. If line 3 is more than line 1, enter -0-.	4		
Taxes You Paid (See page A-2.)	5	State and local income taxes	5		
	6	Real estate taxes (see page A-2)	6	2,200	
	7	Personal property taxes	7	300	
	8	Other taxes. List type and amount ▶	8		
	9	Add lines 5 through 8	9		2,500
Interest You Paid (See page A-3.) Note. Personal interest is not deductible.	10	Home mortgage interest and points reported to you on Form 1098	10		
	11	Home mortgage interest not reported to you on Form 1098. If paid to the person from whom you bought the home, see page A-3 and show that person's name, identifying no., and address ▶	11		
	12	Points not reported to you on Form 1098. See page A-3 for special rules	12		
	13	Investment interest. Attach Form 4952 if required. (See page A-3.)	13		
	14	Add lines 10 through 13	14		
Gifts to Charity If you made a gift and got a benefit for it, see page A-4.	15	Gifts by cash or check. If you made any gift of $250 or more, see page A-4	15	2,400	
	16	Other than by cash or check. If any gift of $250 or more, see page A-4. You must attach Form 8283 if over $500	16		
	17	Carryover from prior year	17		
	18	Add lines 15 through 17	18		2,400
Casualty and Theft Losses	19	Casualty or theft loss(es). Attach Form 4684. (See page A-5.)	19		
Job Expenses and Most Other Miscellaneous Deductions (See page A-5 for expenses to deduct here.)	20	Unreimbursed employee expenses—job travel, union dues, job education, etc. You must attach Form 2106 or 2106-EZ if required. (See page A-5.) ▶	20		
	21	Tax preparation fees	21		
	22	Other expenses—investment, safe deposit box, etc. List type and amount ▶..............................	22		
	23	Add lines 20 through 22	23		
	24	Enter amount from Form 1040, line 36 [24]			
	25	Multiply line 24 by 2% (.02)	25		
	26	Subtract line 25 from line 23. If line 25 is more than line 23, enter -0-	26		
Other Miscellaneous Deductions	27	Other—from list on page A-6. List type and amount ▶ .... Gambling Losses....	27		2,500
Total Itemized Deductions	28	Is Form 1040, line 36, over $137,300 (over $68,650 if married filing separately)? ☐ **No.** Your deduction is not limited. Add the amounts in the far right column for lines 4 through 27. Also, enter this amount on Form 1040, line 38. ☐ **Yes.** Your deduction may be limited. See page A-6 for the amount to enter. } ▶	28		7,400

For Paperwork Reduction Act Notice, see Form 1040 Instructions.   Cat. No. 11330X   Schedule A (Form 1040) 2002

SITUATION 2

Schedules A&B (Form 1040) 2002	OMB No. 1545-0074 Page **2**
Name(s) shown on Form 1040. Do not enter name and social security number if shown on other side.	Your social security number

Schedule B—Interest and Ordinary Dividends

Attachment Sequence No. **08**

**Part I
Interest**

(See page B-1 and the instructions for Form 1040, line 8a.)

1 List name of payer. If any interest is from a seller-financed mortgage and the buyer used the property as a personal residence, see page B-1 and list this interest first. Also, show that buyer's social security number and address ►

	Amount
Local Bank and Trust	800
Local Savings and Loan	1,300
Local Credit Union	400

Note. If you received a Form 1099-INT, Form 1099-OID, or substitute statement from a brokerage firm, list the firm's name as the payer and enter the total interest shown on that form.

2 Add the amounts on line 1	**2**	2,500
3 Excludable interest on series EE and I U.S. savings bonds issued after 1989 from Form 8815, line 14. You **must** attach Form 8815	**3**	
4 Subtract line 3 from line 2. Enter the result here and on Form 1040, line 8a ►	**4**	2,500

Note. If line 4 is over $1,500, you must complete Part III.

**Part II
Ordinary
Dividends**

(See page B-1 and the instructions for Form 1040, line 9.)

5 List name of payer. Include only ordinary dividends. If you received any capital gain distributions, see the instructions for Form 1040, line 13 ►

	Amount
Any Corporation	1,500

Note. If you received a Form 1099-DIV or substitute statement from a brokerage firm, list the firm's name as the payer and enter the ordinary dividends shown on that form.

6 Add the amounts on line 5. Enter the total here and on Form 1040, line 9 . ►	**6**	1,500

Note. If line 6 is over $1,500, you must complete Part III.

**Part III
Foreign
Accounts
and Trusts**

(See page B-2.)

You must complete this part if you **(a)** had over $1,500 of taxable interest or ordinary dividends; OR **(b)** had a foreign account; or **(c)** received a distribution from, or were a grantor of, or a transferor to, a foreign trust.

	Yes	No
7a At any time during 2002, did you have an interest in or a signature or other authority over a financial account in a foreign country, such as a bank account, securities account, or other financial account? See page B-2 for exceptions and filing requirements for Form TD F 90-22.1		
b If "Yes," enter the name of the foreign country ►		
8 During 2002, did you receive a distribution from, or were you the grantor of, or transferor to, a foreign trust? If "Yes," you may have to file Form 3520. See page B-2		

For Paperwork Reduction Act Notice, see Form 1040 instructions.   Schedule B (Form 1040) 2002

SITUATION 2

Social Security Benefits Worksheet—Lines 20a and 20b

Keep for Your Records

Before you begin:	✓ Complete Form 1040, lines 21, 23, and 25 through 31a, if they apply to you.
	✓ Figure any amount to be entered on the dotted line next to line 32 (see page 30).
	✓ If you are married filing separately and you **lived apart** from your spouse for all of 2001, enter "D" to the right of the word "benefits" on line 20a.
	✓ Be sure you have read the **Exception** on page 25 to see if you can use this worksheet instead of a publication to find out if any of your benefits are taxable.

1. Enter the total amount from **box 5** of **all** your **Forms SSA-1099** and RRB-1099 . . . . 1. ___16,500___

2. Is the amount on line 1 more than zero?

　☐ **No. (STOP)** None of your social security benefits are taxable.

　☐ **Yes.** Enter one-half of line 1 . . . . 2. ___8,250___

3. Add the amounts on Form 1040, lines 7, 8a, 9 through 14, 15b, 16b, 17 through 19, and 21. Do not include amounts from box 5 of Forms SSA-1099 or RRB-1099 . . . . 3. ___42,500___

4. Enter the amount, if any, from Form 1040, line 8b . . . . 4. _____

5. Add lines 2, 3, and 4 . . . . 5. ___50,750___

6. Add the amounts on Form 1040, lines 23, and 25 through 31a, and any amount you entered on the dotted line next to line 32 . . . . 6. _____

7. Subtract line 6 from line 5. If zero or less, **stop here.** None of your social security benefits are taxable . . . . 7. ___50,750___

8. Enter: $25,000 if single, head of household, qualifying widow(er), or married filing separately and you **lived apart** from your spouse for all of 2001; $32,000 if married filing jointly; -0- if married filing separately and you lived with your spouse at any time in 2001. . . . . 8. ___32,000___

9. Is the amount on line 8 less than the amount on line 7?

　☐ **No. (STOP)** None of your social security benefits are taxable. You do not have to enter any amounts on lines 20a or 20b of Form 1040. **But if you are married filing separately and you lived apart** from your spouse for all of 2001, enter -0- on line 20b. Be sure you entered "D" to the right of the word "benefits" on line 20a.

　☐ **Yes.** Subtract line 8 from line 7 . . . . 9. ___18,750___

10. Enter: $9,000 if single, head of household, qualifying widow(er), or married filing separately and you **lived apart** from your spouse for all of 2001; $12,000 if married filing jointly; -0- if married filing separately and you lived with your spouse at any time in 2001. . . . . 10. ___12,000___

11. Subtract line 10 from line 9. If zero or less, enter -0- . . . . 11. ___6,750___

12. Enter the **smaller** of line 9 or line 10. . . . . 12. ___12,000___

13. Enter one-half of line 12 . . . . 13. ___6,000___

14. Enter the **smaller** of line 2 or line 13. . . . . 14. ___6,000___

15. Multiply line 11 by 85% (.85). If line 11 is zero, enter -0- . . . . 15. ___5,738___

16. Add lines 14 and 15. . . . . 16. ___11,738___

17. Multiply line 1 by 85% (.85). . . . . 17. ___14,025___

18. **Taxable social security benefits.** Enter the **smaller** of line 16 or line 17 . . . . . . 18. ___11,738___

　● Enter the amount from line 1 above on Form 1040, line 20a.

　● Enter the amount from line 18 above on Form 1040, line 20b.

 TIP If part of your benefits are taxable for 2001 **and** they include benefits paid in 2001 that were for an earlier year, you may be able to reduce the taxable amount. See Pub. 915 for details.

SUMMARY

In the case of John and Jane Taxpayer, adding $2,500 of gambling winnings to their total income had the following effect:

- It increased the taxable portion of their Social Security by $2,125.
- It did not increase their standard/itemized deduction amount since their itemized deductions, including the gambling losses, did not exceed the standard deduction they were entitled to.
- Even though their winnings equaled their losses, they still increased their total tax liability from $4,764 to $5,458.

Naturally, the results will be different for each taxpayer. If you have gambling winnings during the year, you should review your tax situation carefully. You may even want to consider making estimated quarterly payments to avoid problems at the end of the year.

Above all, don't assume that gambling losses will automatically offset gains, or that they won't affect your tax liability.

11

◆

Filing an Amended Tax Return

Had John and Jane Taxpayer filed their return and then discovered that they had omitted their gambling winnings and losses, they would have been required to file an amended tax return Form 1040X.

Form 1040X is required only after the original return has been filed. Generally, Form 1040X must be filed within three years of the date the original return was filed, and should be mailed to the Internal Revenue Service Center where the original return was sent.

A separate Form 1040X is required for each year being amended. When an amended federal return is needed, an amended state return may also be required.

Had they neglected to report their gambling activity, John and Jane Taxpayer would have filed Form 1040X, which appears on the next two pages.

| Form **1040X** (Rev. November 2001) | | Department of the Treasury—Internal Revenue Service
Amended U.S. Individual Income Tax Return
▶ See separate instructions. | | OMB No. 1545-0091 |

This return is for calendar year ▶   2002   , or fiscal year ended ▶

Please print or type

Your first name and initial JOHN	Last name TAXPAYER	Your social security number 001 : 01 : 0001
If a joint return, spouse's first name and initial JANE	Last name TAXPAYER	Spouse's social security number 002 : 01 : 0002
Home address (no. and street) or P.O. box if mail is not delivered to your home 123 ANY STREET	Apt. no.	Phone number ( )
City, town or post office, state, and ZIP code. If you have a foreign address, see page 2 of the instructions. ANYWHERE PA 00001		For Paperwork Reduction Act Notice, see page 6.

A   If the name or address shown above is different from that shown on the original return, check here . . . . ▶ ☐

B   Has the original return been changed or audited by the IRS or have you been notified that it will be? . . . ☐ Yes ☒ No

C   Filing status. Be sure to complete this line. **Note.** You cannot change from joint to separate returns after the due date.

On original return ▶ ☐ Single ☒ Married filing joint return ☐ Married filing separate return ☐ Head of household ☐ Qualifying widow(er)

On this return ▶ ☐ Single ☒ Married filing joint return ☐ Married filing separate return ☐ Head of household* ☐ Qualifying widow(er)

* If the qualifying person is a child but not your dependent, see page 2.

Use Part II on the Back to Explain any Changes		**A.** Original amount or as previously adjusted (see page 2)	**B.** Net change— amount of increase or (decrease)— explain in Part II	**C.** Correct amount
Income and Deductions (see pages 2–6)				
1 Adjusted gross income (see page 3)	1	49,613	4,625	54,238
2 Itemized deductions or standard deduction (see page 3). .	2	7,850		7,850
3 Subtract line 2 from line 1	3	41,763	4,625	46,388
4 Exemptions. If changing, fill in Parts I and II on the back .	4	6,000		6,000
5 Taxable income. Subtract line 4 from line 3	5	35,763	4,625	40,388
6 Tax (see page 4). Method used in col. C **TAX RATES**	6	4,764	694	5,458
7 Credits (see page 4)	7			
8 Subtract line 7 from line 6. Enter the result but not less than zero .	8	4,764	694	5,458
9 Other taxes (see page 4)	9			
10 Total tax. Add lines 8 and 9	10	4,764	694	5,458
11 Federal income tax withheld and excess social security and RRTA tax withheld. If changing, see page 4	11	5,200		5,200
12 Estimated tax payments, including amount applied from prior year's return	12			
13 Earned income credit (EIC)	13			
14 Additional child tax credit from Form 8812	14			
15 Credits from Form 2439 or Form 4136	15			
16 Amount paid with request for extension of time to file (see page 4)			16	
17 Amount of tax paid with original return plus additional tax paid after it was filed			17	
18 Total payments. Add lines 11 through 17 in column C			18	5,200
Refund or Amount You Owe				
19 Overpayment, if any, as shown on original return or as previously adjusted by the IRS . . .			19	436
20 Subtract line 19 from line 18 (see page 5)			20	4,764
21 **Amount you owe.** If line 10, column C, is more than line 20, enter the difference and see page 5 . .			21	694
22 If line 10, column C, is less than line 20, enter the difference			22	
23 Amount of line 22 you want **refunded to you**			23	
24 Amount of line 22 you want **applied to your** **estimated tax** 24				

Sign Here

Joint return? See page 2. Keep a copy for your records.

Under penalties of perjury, I declare that I have filed an original return and that I have examined this amended return, including accompanying schedules and statements, and to the best of my knowledge and belief, this amended return is true, correct, and complete. Declaration of preparer (other than taxpayer) is based on all information of which the preparer has any knowledge.

Your signature	Date	Spouse's signature. If a joint return, both must sign.	Date

Paid Preparer's Use Only

Preparer's signature	Date	Check if self-employed ☐	Preparer's SSN or PTIN
Firm's name (or yours if self-employed), address, and ZIP code ▶		EIN Phone no. ( )	

Cat. No. 11360L   Form **1040X** (Rev. 11-2001)

Filing an Amended Tax Return

65

Form 1040X (Rev. 11-2001)   Page 2

Part I — Exemptions. See Form 1040 or 1040A instructions.

If you are **not changing your exemptions,** do not complete this part.
If claiming **more exemptions,** complete lines 25–31.
If claiming **fewer exemptions,** complete lines 25–30.

		A. Original number of exemptions reported or as previously adjusted	B. Net change	C. Correct number of exemptions
25	Yourself and spouse			
	Caution. If your parents (or someone else) can claim you as a dependent (even if they chose not to), you cannot claim an exemption for yourself.			
26	Your dependent children who lived with you			
27	Your dependent children who did not live with you due to divorce or separation			
28	Other dependents			
29	Total number of exemptions. Add lines 25 through 28			
30	Multiply the number of exemptions claimed on line 29 by the amount listed below for the tax year you are amending. Enter the result here and on line 4.			

Tax year	Exemption amount	But see the instructions for line 4 on page 3 if the amount on line 1 is over:
2001	$2,900	$99,725
2000	2,800	96,700
1999	2,750	94,975
1998	2,700	93,400

30

31   Dependents (children and other) not claimed on original (or adjusted) return:

(a) First name Last name	(b) Dependent's social security number	(c) Dependent's relationship to you	(d) ✓ if qualifying child for child tax credit (see page 5)
			☐
			☐
			☐
			☐
			☐

No. of your children on line 31 who:
- lived with you . . ▶ ☐
- did not live with you due to divorce or separation (see page 5) . ▶ ☐

Dependents on line 31 not entered above ▶ ☐

Part II — Explanation of Changes to Income, Deductions, and Credits

Enter the line number from the front of the form for each item you are changing and give the reason for each change. Attach only the supporting forms and schedules for the items changed. If you do not attach the required information, your Form 1040X may be returned. Be sure to include your name and social security number on any attachments.

If the change relates to a net operating loss carryback or a general business credit carryback, attach the schedule or form that shows the year in which the loss or credit occurred. See page 2 of the instructions. Also, check here . . . . . . ▶ ☐

LINE 1 - INCREASED TO INCLUDE GAMBLING WINNINGS   2,500

INCREASED TO INCLUDE ADDITIONAL TAXABLE SOCIAL SECURITY BENEFITS   2,125

TOTAL - LINE 1 - B - NET CHANGE   4,625

Part III — Presidential Election Campaign Fund. Checking below will not increase your tax or reduce your refund.

If you did not previously want $3 to go to the fund but now want to, check here . . . . ▶ ☐
If a joint return and your spouse did not previously want $3 to go to the fund but now wants to, check here . . . . ▶ ☐

Form **1040X** (Rev. 11-2001)

12

$\blacklozenge$

What's New

Each edition of *The Gambler's Guide to Taxes* will include current issues related to gaming being addressed at the federal level. This edition focuses on Act 5301, Internal Revenue Code Section 451, one of seven acts introduced in Congress and the report of the National Gambling Impact Study Commission.

ACT 5301: INTERNAL REVENUE CODE
SECTION 451

The Act provides that a prizewinner who is provided the option to choose cash or annuity within sixty days after being entitled to the prize is not required to include amounts in gross income, merely by reason of having the option. Types of prizes qualifying are lotteries, jackpots, games or similar arrangements that provide a series of payments over a period of at least ten years provided that the prize or award does not relate to any past services performed by the recipient and does not require the recipient to perform any substantial future services.

The provision is effective for prizes to which the taxpayer first became entitled after October 21, 1998. The provision also applies to a prize to which the taxpayer became entitled before October 21, 1998, if the taxpayer has the option to receive a single cash payment during the eighteen-month period beginning on July 1, 1999.

NATIONAL GAMBLING IMPACT STUDY

The 104th Congress through Public Law 104169 signed by President Clinton on August 3, 1996, created the National Gambling Impact Study Commission. For two years, the Commission conducted a comprehensive legal and factual study of the social and economic impacts of gambling on federal, state, local, and Native American tribal governments; and on communities and social institutions. On June 18, 1999, the Commission released their report containing over seventy recommendations to Congress, the President and the governors.

The results of the Commission are best summarized in the 106th Congress concurrent resolution (H.Con.Res.137) as follows:

Expressing the sense of Congress with regard to the recommendations of the National Gambling Impact Study Commission.

Whereas the National Gambling Impact Study Commission was established August 3, 1996, under Public Law 104-169;

Whereas the Commission was charged with the responsibility of conducting a comprehensive legal and factual study of the social and economic impacts of legalized gambling in the United States, including the impacts on communities, social institutions, and individuals, as well as the role of government;

Whereas the Commission officially began its two-year study on June 18, 1997, and released its report and findings on June 18, 1999;

Whereas the Commission found that 5.4 million adult Americans are pathological or problem gamblers and 15.4 million more adult Americans are considered at-risk gamblers with a high potential for becoming problem gamblers, and further reported that 7.9 million adolescent Americans are pathological or problem gamblers;

Whereas the Commission found that gambling disproportionately impacts the most vulnerable Americans—the working poor, the elderly population, and our Nation's youth;

Whereas the Commission found that the cost of gambling is conservatively estimated at $6 billion per year, without factoring in the immeasurable, but most devastating, social costs associated with gambling, such as child abuse, suicide, and other destructive impacts of gambling on individuals and families;

Whereas the Commission determined that unregulated growth of the gambling industry is seen as a dangerous course of action;

Whereas the Commission determined that the more Americans are presented with opportunities to gamble, the more concern there is about problem and pathological gambling, and that the social, legal, and financial consequences of pathological gambling addiction are severe;

Whereas the Commission determined that technology is revolutionizing the gambling industry, and that Internet gambling in particular poses serious legal, economic, and social concerns which the Nation is not prepared to deal with;

Whereas the Commission determined that many policymakers have been forced to make decisions about expanding gambling with virtually no credible studies to rely on and, at best, only an assessment of the perceived social impacts;

Whereas the Commission recommended that Congress adopt a general research strategy to build a knowledge of gambling behavior and its consequences on individuals and communities, which would add "gambling components" to existing data sets being collected by Federal agencies and national institutes on related areas;

Whereas the Commission recommended that Congress authorize the National Science Foundation to establish a multidisciplinary research program on the social and economic impacts of legal gambling in the United States, including the benefits associated with legalized gambling as well as its costs;

Whereas the Commission recommended that governors and State legislatures:

(1) authorize and fund every four years an objective study on the prevalence of problem and pathological gamblers among their State's residents;

(2) fund research, public awareness education, prevention and treatment programs for those who are, or are likely to become problem or pathological gamblers among their resident population; and

(3) as a condition of the granting of a license to operate a gambling facility, or to sell goods or services to a gambling facility, provide full cooperation in any research undertaken by the State needed to fulfill the legislative intent of Federal and State statutory policy;

Whereas the Commission recommended that the States with lotteries publicly develop and review model regulations for their lotteries;

Whereas the Commission recommended the funding of educational and prevention programs to help the public recognize that almost all sports gambling is illegal and can have serious consequences;

Whereas the Commission recommended the adoption of enforceable advertising guidelines for the gambling industry, particularly as they relate to youths and low-income neighborhoods;

Whereas the Commission recommended the development of a strategy to prohibit Internet gambling within the United States;

Whereas the Commission recommended that Congress direct the National Institute of Justice to research the effects of gambling on property and crime; and

Whereas the members of the Commission unanimously recommended a "pause" in the growth of gambling, to give governments further time to research and assess the impact of gambling: Now, therefore, be it

Resolved by the House of Representatives (the Senate concurring), That Congress encourages Federal, State, local, and tribal governments to review the findings of the National Gambling Impact Study Commission, and to consider the implementation of its recommendations as an appropriate response to the many concerns brought about by the rapid acceleration of gambling in our society.

ACTIVITY OF THE 107TH CONGRESS

The following bills related to gaming activity have been introduced during the 107th Congress. If you have a particular interest in a specific bill you should contact either your Representative or Senator.

H.R. 2572: Gambling ATM and Credit/Debit Card Reform Act

To implement certain recommendations of the National Gambling Impact Study Commission by prohibiting the placement of automated teller machines or any device by which an extension of credit or electronic fund transfer may be initiated by a consumer in the immediate area in a gambling establishment where gambling or wagering takes place.

H.R. 556: Unlawful Internet Gambling Funding Prohibition Act

To prevent the use of certain bank instruments for unlawful Internet gambling, and for other purposes. No person engaged in a gambling business may knowingly accept, in connection with the participation of another person in unlawful Internet gambling:

(1) credit, or the proceeds of credit, extended to or on behalf of such other person (including credit extended through the use of a credit card);

(2) an electronic fund transfer or funds transmitted by or through a money transmitting business, or the proceeds of an electronic fund transfer or money transmitting service, from or on behalf of the other person;

(3) any check, draft, or similar instrument which is drawn by or on behalf of the other person and is drawn on or payable at or through any financial institution; or

(4) the proceeds of any other form of financial transaction as the Secretary may prescribe by regulation which involves a financial institution as a payer or financial intermediary on behalf of or for the benefit of the other person.

H.R. 3215: Combating Illegal Gambling Reform and Modernization Act

To amend Title 18, United States Code, to expand and modernize the prohibition against interstate gambling.

H.R. 338: National Collegiate and Amateur Protection Act of 2001

To protect amateur athletics and combat illegal sports gambling.

The act would establish a prosecutorial task force on illegal wagering on amateur and collegiate sporting events.

The task force shall:

(1) coordinate enforcement of Federal laws that prohibit gambling related to amateur and collegiate events; and

(2) submit annually, to the House of Representatives and the Senate a report describing specific violations of such laws, prosecutions commenced, and convictions obtained.

H.R. 641: National Collegiate and Amateur Athletic Protection Act of 2001

See details for S. 338

S. 718: Amateur Integrity Act

Section 201 of this Act prohibits gambling on competitive games involving high school and college athletes and the Olympics.

H.R. 110: Student Athlete Protection Act

To prohibit high school and college sports gambling in all states including states where gambling was permitted prior to 1991.

Part II

SELECTED ARTICLES

13

◆

Is It Gaming or Gambling?

Queen Anne of England Settles the Debate

by Basil Nestor, author of
The Unofficial Guide to Casino Gambling

I was poking around the Net recently (checking on the stock market, the ultimate casino) when I came across this archived letter to the editor at Money.com:

> In the May 3 (1999) Money Daily I see you have taken up the gambling industry's favorite euphemism for their activity— namely "gaming" instead of "gambling." Surely you know that this euphemism is simply a product of the gambling industry's PR machine, and that its purpose is to disguise the reality of the activity. A game is only just a game if it puts nothing of substance at risk. Gambling, on the other hand, is staking something valuable on chance. Please stick with the real word, "gambling," and avoid the Orwellian newspeak being pushed on us by the gambling industry. MK.

Five minutes later I read this on a journalist's Web page. It was titled "Weasel Words":

> Whenever you write about gambling in your stories do not— NOT—write "gaming" (as in "The gaming corporation estimates revenues from VLT gaming at $100 million a year")

unless you're directly quoting an industry spokesperson. They
want us to use "gaming" instead of "gambling" because it
sounds more innocuous, as if to say, "It's just a game and people are having fun." But it's gambling, and we owe it to our
readers to remind them of that.

It's everywhere, a perennial argument, a kind of urban myth that
has a life of its own, much like the myth about people who are
drugged and have their kidneys stolen. Legislators, antigaming activ-
ists, even reporters (who are supposed to be informed) pass this tru-
ism along. They tell us that the word "gaming" is a PR ploy, an
insidious linguistic invention created to soften the negative impres-
sions of "gambling."
Well, guess what? They're all wrong! It's the other way around.
"Gambling" is a word that was invented to besmirch "gaming"!

GAMING CAME FIRST

Yes, that wonderfully fun thing we do with cards, dice, and wheels
was called "gaming" way back when English was being cobbled together from the French, German, and Anglo-Saxon tongues. The
roots of the word extend into the medieval depths of the twelfth century. It started as *gaman* in Old High German, and it meant "amuse-
ment." The word morphed into *gamen* in Old English, and it had been
"gaming" for centuries by the time Shakespeare used it in *Hamlet*. In
Act 3, Scene 3, the young prince considers murdering his uncle, but
the older man is praying. Hamlet decides it would be better to skewer
him when he is "at gaming, swearing, or about some act that has no
relish of salvation in't."
"Gambling" had not yet been conceived as a word when the English adopted the Statute of Anne (named for Britain's then reigning
queen) in 1710. The statute says:

> [A]ll notes, bills, bonds, judgments, mortgages, or other secu-
> rities or conveyances . . . or other valuable thing whatsoever,
> won by gaming or playing at cards, dice, tables, tennis, bowls,
> or other game or games whatsoever, or by betting . . . shall be

utterly void, frustrate, and of none effect, to all intents and purposes whatsoever . . .

In other words, gaming debts were not collectible. By the way, The Statute of Anne is more than just a musty relic of history. It's a part of common law, and thus still on the books to this very day. Gaming debts are not collectible in most states. Nevada didn't get around to modifying this basic rule until 1983. But hey, that's an interesting subject for another article.

GAMBLING AND GAMBLERS

Continuing with our story, the first incarnation of the word "gambling" was "gambler." It appeared in the early eighteenth century, and it was originally considered to be coarse slang. The lexicographer Samuel Johnson described "gambler" as "a cant word, I suppose, for game or gamester." "Cant" was the jargon of thieves and beggars, so gambling had a negative meaning from the very beginning. Johnson tells us that a gambler was "a knave whose practice it is to invite the unwary to game and cheat them."

This distinction between an honest game and a dishonest, unfair gamble quickly took hold. Gentlemen were gamesters; knaves and their victims were gamblers. And so, Ralph Waldo Emerson could write: "The cheat, the defaulter, the gambler, cannot extort the knowledge of material and moral nature which his honest care and pains yield to the operative." But Emerson also wrote: "The end and the means, the gamester and the game, —life is made up of the intermixture and reaction of these two amicable powers . . ."

George Washington's general orders of January 27, 1780, contain another example of this dual meaning:

By the same Court, Captain Prince of the 2nd Maryland regiment was tried for 'Gaming with Cards for money,' for 'Neglect of duty, Gambling, Behaving in a manner unbecoming the character of an officer . . .'

Apparently, "gaming" was different enough from "gambling" to require a separate charge. And "gaming" certainly didn't mean playing for fun. Washington's orders of January 8, 1778, clearly demonstrate that it meant wagering:

> The Commander in Chief is informed that gaming is again creeping into the Army; in a more especial manner among the lower staff in the environs of the camp. He therefore in the most solemn terms declares, that this Vice in either Officer or soldier, shall not when detected, escape exemplary punishment; and to avoid discrimination between play and gaming forbids Cards and Dice under any pretence whatsoever.

Of course, the degree of the vice tended to depend on one's point of view. George Washington also played card games for money, and his journals are filled with entries documenting his wins and losses. Furthermore, public lotteries helped fund the Revolution.

This obvious and untenable contradiction slowly pushed "gaming" and "gambling" closer together in meaning, but they never quite merged because one person's fair game for small stakes might be another person's crooked game for large stakes. The definition remained relative, and so the two words lurched on through the nineteenth century like unhappy companions handcuffed together.

In 1816, Thomas Jefferson referred to gamblers in the most unpleasant terms, but it wasn't gamesters he was criticizing:

> The system of banking . . . I contemplate it as a blot left in all our constitutions, which, if not covered, will end in their destruction, which is already hit by the gamblers in corruption, and is sweeping away in its progress the fortunes and morals of our citizens.

And an organization called the Anti-Gambling Association still referred to wagering as gaming in 1891: "Before the third crusade, there was no check upon the gaming vice, and no limit to the stakes."

GAMBLING BECOMES THE "G" WORD

So, how did gambling get the upper hand? Why do so many people perceive gaming to be a slick invention of the late twentieth century?

The cause for the switch can be found in the Victorian sensibilities that swept through the English-speaking world in the late nineteenth century, and it was pushed along greatly by serious corruption that infested many forms of gaming at that time. Even some government-sponsored lotteries were crooked, most especially the infamous Louisiana lottery (sometimes referred to as "The Serpent"). People were tired of being swindled. When the temperance movement picked up steam at the turn of the last century, gam(bl)ing went the way of alcohol. Organized wagering disappeared from the realm of legal and legitimate society. The options became cards with your friends (which led to an explosion in the popularity of poker), or the "private" casino down the street. And who ran that casino? They were no longer called "knaves." The new word was "gangster," and walking into one of those joints was *definitely* a gamble.

Even after Nevada legalized gaming in 1931, casinos remained illegal elsewhere for nearly another half-century. That gave organized crime an unfortunate advantage. Unsavory characters like Ben "Bugsy" Siegel funneled investment money from criminal gambling operations in other states to legal properties in Nevada, and then profits were skimmed and sent back to the investors. Anyone who was reasonably well-informed knew that playing in a casino often meant wagering with organized crime. It didn't matter that the casino bosses wore expensive, tailored suits, or that a famous entertainer was performing in the lounge, or even that the game was probably honest (though it sometimes wasn't). There was no getting around the fact that you were playing roulette in a mob-owned establishment. Win or lose, your mom would not be pleased. Buddy, you were gambling!

Meanwhile, that other, gentler word kept chugging along. "Gaming" continued to be used as a literal and exact description of the act of wagering. Gaming is what the industry was called. Gaming is what regulators were regulating when they ejected the Mob in the latter half of the last century. The perception that the word "gaming" appeared suddenly is entirely due to the growing popularity of casinos. Many U.S. citizens grew up hearing the word "gambling," and they're just now being exposed to the older term "gaming." That's why I titled my latest book the *Unofficial Guide to Casino Gambling;* I wanted everyone to instantly understand what it is about.

There's no doubt that "gambling" still carries a bit of a stigma in some circles, and "gaming" certainly sounds a tad more refined and upper-crust, but one word is not necessarily more genuine than the other, and "gaming" is certainly not a "weasel word." At this point in history, the two words are practically synonymous, though purists would certainly remind us that the Statute of Anne still carries the force of law, so gaming has a bit of an edge over gambling in absolute legitimacy.

Let's face it, we could call it "fitzfuzzling" and it wouldn't change a thing. It's still a game played for money, so our goal should be to play the best game, whatever we call it.

14

◆

Gambling and Taxes

by Professor I. Nelson Rose

Gamblers are notorious for being flush one day, and broke the next. If you happen to be in the chips when April 15 rolls around, you just hire a tax expert to fill out the forms and write the IRS a check. If, on the other hand, the cards haven't been falling your way, you can get an extension on filing the forms, but no leeway is given on paying Uncle Sam his share.

Just what is his share of your winnings? Or losses, for that matter? Although the tax laws can be very complicated and unfair, the courts, and even the IRS, have given gamblers some breaks, if they are smart enough to take advantage of them.

It is possible for a gambler to take both losses and expenses off his taxes. A recent Supreme Court case held that a player who treats his gambling like a full-time job is entitled to all of the tax breaks of any other trade or business. If you are a casual gambler, however, you cannot deduct your travel and other expenses, and your gambling losses are limited to the amount of your winnings.

Are these really restrictions? Yes and no. Since you are limited to the amount you won in any year, the tax laws obviously hurt you if you have a losing year and don't help you very much if you make a big win. On the other hand, there is nothing that limits the losses you can deduct to any one session, or any one type of game, or even to legal gambling.

If you win $30,000 over the course of the year, but lose $35,000 total, you are supposed to report the $30,000 as part of your gross earnings and then take only $30,000 (not the full $35,000) as an itemized deduction. If your losses had been from speculation in the stock or commodities markets instead of "gambling," or you are a professional gambler, you are able to report the entire $35,000 loss.

A winning year for the casual gambler is a little better, but not much. If you win $35,000 over the course of the year and lose $30,000 total, you report the $35,000 as income and then take the $30,000 off as a deduction. The professional gambler or stock market speculator is in the same boat, with one extra advantage—if the professional gambler had a big loss from the previous year, he could carry the loss forward and take it off his taxes this year; the casual gambler must treat each year separately and losses not used in any tax year are gone forever.

Of course, winning is only important for tax purposes if the IRS finds out about it. Technically, every nickel you win from a slot machine is supposed to be reported as income. Even the IRS is smart enough to figure out that practically nobody would report any of their winnings. So, the IRS puts the burden on the payor: the casino, race track, or lottery.

Say you win a major tournament for $100,000. The casino is required to report your big win to the IRS, on Form 1099 Misc. Assuming you are on a regular calendar year for your tax year, as most people are, you can deduct all of your gambling losses from that year off your taxable income, up to $100,000. If you win on January 2, you will have 363 days to accumulate and prove gambling losses.

What do you do if you win big on December 23? You could scramble, sweep up losing tickets off the track grounds, get your friends to say they won thousands from you earlier that year, or various other schemes that are not only illegal, but universally unsuccessful. What you should be doing, what you should have done throughout the year, is to keep detailed records and an accurate diary of your winnings and losses every single time you gamble so that you can substantiate your claim that you had lost many times during the previous eleven months.

And remember, you are not limited to the type of gambling loss you can deduct. From your big win at the track you can deduct losses from casinos, home poker games, and even illegal sports bets with bookies. The IRS cannot turn this information over to any other prosecutor (and the bet may not have been illegal anyway; sometimes only the bookie is breaking the law, not the player).

Of course, no gambling loss does you any good if you cannot prove it to the IRS or ultimately to a judge. What type of records should you keep? The IRS would have you keep books more detailed than a businessman's expense account. You are advised to keep permanent books of accounts or records with the names of other players and lots of other documents that no gambler usually gets or keeps.

The IRS and the courts are hard on gamblers trying to prove losses. Losing tickets from the track will be checked for scuff marks from being stepped on and will be run through computers to see if the bettor could have really made the bets claimed. The ink in a gambler's notebook will be checked to verify the dates losing entries were made.

A taxpayer who kept no detailed records found that his quick notebook entries of net gambling winnings were admissible, but entries showing net losses were disregarded as "self-serving declarations." Other courts, however, have allowed gambling losses where the gambler kept cancelled checks, ticket stubs, and a detailed and accurate record book. One taxpayer was allowed a deduction for all gambling losses in his monthly diary because he had included all race-track winnings in the diary, even those that were not reported by the track on the track's withholding form.

The best way to prove gambling losses is to keep meticulous and accurate records of all gaming sessions with supporting documentation. Keep a diary of your gambling, including place, amount won or lost, and bet, and any other information that will substantiate that you actually made the bet. Write your notes during or immediately after each session.

A good poker player or handicapper keeps records like this anyway, why not a player of blackjack, craps, or even the slots? Get a big manila envelope and throw in any receipts, money orders, cancelled checks, hotel bills, markers, or anything else related to the gambling session. You don't have to be neat. And for big losses, get a statement from the pit boss or casino.

And if you are a full-time gambler, you are in luck. The Supreme Court recently opened the door for you to save additional thousands off your taxes. In a recent surprise ruling, the Court decided that gambling is not always sin and corruption; sometimes it is a business.

If you are a full-time gambler, the Supreme Court has now given you a choice. For most gamblers, it would probably pay to declare yourself in the trade or business of professional gambling.

You could then take expenses off, such as all of your travel, meals, and hotel bills, etc., as well as the cost of my book *Gambling and the Law,* which contains more gambling tax information. You could set up a Keogh retirement account and deduct those contributions from your taxes.

On the other hand, declaring yourself a professional gambler might subject you to self-employment taxes. But if being in the trade or business of gambling would result in more, rather than less, taxes, simply go out of "business" and remain a casual gambler.

To get the new tax breaks, you must devote full-time to your business, which I interpret to be at least six to eight hours a day, five days a week. Card counters, pro poker players, handicappers, and "prop" players should qualify.

The actual case decided by the Supreme Court involved a gambler with no other job, but I don't think that is a requirement. Interestingly, this gambler showed a net loss at the end of the year, proving that you do not have to be a winner to be a pro.

However, this is not for the casual bettor. As the high court put it:

> We accept the fact that to be engaged in a trade or business, the taxpayer must be involved in the activity with continuity and regularity and that the taxpayer's primary purpose for engaging in the activity must be for income or profit. A sporadic activity, a hobby, or an amusement diversion does not qualify.

In addition, you must keep detailed, accurate records and receipts. Remember, this isn't just a game—you are now the professional.

15

◆

Taxes and the Lottery

by Roy Lewis

Many people, myself included, consider the lottery to be little more than a tax on the ill informed. There are so many other games of chance and skill where the odds aren't stacked so greatly against you. But, from time to time, some of you are lucky enough to win a shilling or two in your favorite lottery. How will that impact you and your taxes? Let's take a quick look. Here's a brief rundown on the tax implications of winning the lottery.

HOW LOTTERY WINNINGS ARE TAXED

First, you should be aware that your lottery winnings are taxable. This is the case for cash winnings and for the fair market value of any noncash prizes you might win (e.g., a car, vacation, etc.). Depending on your other income and the amount of your winnings, your federal tax bracket can go as high as 38.6 percent.

Your lottery winnings might also be subject to state income tax. Thus, depending on where you live, your total tax bill could exceed 50 percent. You don't get any capital gains rate break for lottery winnings, nor is there any income averaging to help lower your tax bill. In short, you're stuck. But you can be happy knowing that money won is much sweeter than money earned. And paying taxes on money won is a bit easier to deal with than paying taxes on those wages that you work so hard to generate. But let's also see if there are ways that we can take a bicuspid out of that tax bite.

GAMBLING LOSSES

You're entitled to a tax deduction for any gambling losses you had. These are taken as an itemized deduction, but your losses *can't exceed your winnings*. In other words, if you report no gambling income, you'll get no benefit of gambling deductions. Gambling losses aren't subject to the 2 percent floor on miscellaneous itemized deductions, nor are they subject to the 3–80 percent overall limitation on itemized deductions. When you gamble and lose, you should keep the documentary evidence of your ticket purchases (cancelled checks, credit card charges, losing tickets, etc.). In some cases, taxpayer estimates have been allowed, but you shouldn't rely on this—documentary evidence is preferable by far.

But another tip that many fail to consider when they take their lottery winnings over a number of years: that those future payments are also considered gambling winnings . . . which will allow for the deduction of gambling losses in future years. In other words, the payout to you will be considered gambling winnings regardless of whether you receive them in one lump sum or paid out over a number of years. And, since you must have gambling winnings in order to deduct your gambling losses, you would have "built-in" winnings for the next ten or twenty years from a lottery payoff that you elect to take in annual installments.

One final warning on gambling deductions: They might not be all they're cracked up to be. You can't simply "net out" your winnings and losses and report that net figure on the front of your tax return. Instead, you must report your entire winnings as income, and use your losses as itemized deductions. But what if you don't have any other itemized deductions? Will your gambling losses do you any good? Perhaps not . . . since your standard deduction will be greater than your gambling losses, which will yield you *no additional* tax deduction. But the winnings might have a significant impact on your total taxes and may cause you to pay additional taxes (such as making some of your Social Security earnings taxable when they otherwise wouldn't be). So don't automatically think of your gambling losses as a tax-savings vehicle. For many folks, they just aren't.

WHEN LOTTERY WINNINGS ARE TAXED

You report the income in the year, or years, the winnings are received. In the case of noncash prizes, this would be the year the prize is received. In the case of cash winnings, the year you report the winnings would depend on whether the lottery prize is payable in installments, or you are given the option to elect payment in one lump sum.

If a state lottery prize is payable in installments, you must include the annual payments and any amount designated as interest on the unpaid installments as income when received. If you elect to receive payment of a state lottery prize in a lump sum, you must include the entire lump sum in income in the year received.

In any case, the controlling time to report the winnings is when you actually receive them, regardless of when you might have won them. Consider the lucky person who wins the lottery in December 2001, but because of delays in presenting the ticket to authorities and administrative time to actually issue the payment, the check was not given to the winner until January 2002. Despite that the actual win took place in 2001, the income isn't reported until 2002 . . . when the money was actually received.

And, if you think about it, this could work to your benefit. If you can push your winnings into a future tax year, you might actually pay fewer taxes simply because it'll give you time to manage your affairs in that future year to minimize other income (like the wages from your job, which you'll likely immediately quit). So be sure to make some tax-smart decisions when the time comes to cash in your lottery winnings.

WITHHOLDING

If you win more than $5,000 in the lottery, 27 percent must be withheld from your winnings for federal income tax purposes. You will receive a Form W-2G from the payor showing the amount of lottery winnings paid to you during the year and the amount of federal income tax withheld. (This information also gets sent to the IRS by the payor.)

You must give the payor your Social Security number, and the payor might use Form W-9 to request this information from you. If you fail to give the payor your Social Security number, 31 percent will be withheld.

If state income tax withholding is required, the amount of state income tax withheld might also be shown on form W-2G.

ESTIMATED TAXES

Since your federal tax bracket can go as high as 38.6 percent, which is well above the 27 percent they will withhold for large winnings, the amount of tax withheld from your lottery winnings might not necessarily be enough to cover your tax bill. On top of your regular tax liability, you could be assessed an additional penalty for failure to make estimated tax payments during the year. Thus, you might also have to make estimated tax payments in advance. So, if you think this might apply to you, make sure you understand the rules about prepaying your taxes. But, more important, there are loopholes that you can use when you don't pay your taxes in advance: pay them all on April 15 and avoid any penalties or interest. So while you're looking into the estimated tax rules, make sure you check out the estimated tax-penalty exceptions.

ASSIGNMENT OF LOTTERY TICKETS

If you are sharing the winnings, you could still wind up paying tax on the entire amount, depending on the sharing agreement. The key is to establish that the assignment of all or part of a lottery ticket took place before you won. That is, if you simply win and then give away part of the winnings, you will be taxed on the full amount and will be treated as having made a separate gift (which, depending on whom you gave it to and the amount, could itself be subject to gift tax).

But, if you and another individual(s) agree to share the ticket before it turns out to be a winner, then you each report only your share in income. Note that if the person you claim to have shared the ticket with is a family member, the IRS might question the validity of the sharing agreement.

ASSIGNMENT OF LOTTERY WINNINGS PAYABLE IN INSTALLMENTS FOR LUMP SUM

Several companies are in the business of acquiring lottery winnings that are payable in installments from prizewinners in exchange for a discounted lump sum. If you assign your right to future lottery installments to one of these companies for a lump sum in an arm's length transaction, the assignment is treated as a sale. You would have to include the lump sum as income in the year of the sale. And just because we're calling this transaction a "sale," don't think that you'll receive capital gains tax treatment (and a lower tax rate) on this "sale." The IRS would treat this transaction as nothing more than a discounted present value of an ordinary income stream. That being the case, the "sale" would produce ordinary income, and would not be considered a sale of a capital asset.

DIVORCE SITUATIONS

If a divorce court requires a lottery winner to turn over a portion of the periodic lottery winnings to his or her spouse, the lottery winner must take great care to insure that the court recognized the winner's tax burden when deciding how much should be turned over.

In one case, for example, a lottery winner agreed to turn over half of his yearly lottery payments to his ex-spouse, but neglected to take into account that he still had to pay income taxes on the entire amount of each installment he received. If you find yourself in divorce proceedings and are still playing the lottery (is this called "double jeopardy"?), be very, very careful.

ESTATE TAX

If you win a very large amount, the proceeds might be payable over a period of years—for example, equal payments over twenty years. If you die early in the payment period, the present value of the proceeds payable after your death would be includable in your estate, but your estate might not have the cash to pay the tax on that includable amount.

Proper planning can avoid this problem. If you are fortunate enough to win a sizable lottery prize, I strongly recommend that you review your entire estate plan.

Or, you can make your life much easier and simply give the ticket to me. ☺

16

◆

Winnings and the Tax Man

by Professor I. Nelson Rose

In the old ABC television show *Lottery!*, a U.S. Internal Revenue Service special agent accompanied the lottery representative who merrily handed out envelopes filled with multimillion dollar checks. Although the IRS's presence on the show was probably only a device to keep the plots going (after all, a lottery agent doesn't get to carry a gun, but an IRS agent does), the show greatly underestimated the government's ingenuity and resources.

Can the IRS have a man stationed in every casino and card room full-time? At every horse and dog track? In every state lottery every day? And since even illegal winnings are taxable, can the IRS be at every big-stakes poker game, in every bookie joint, and following every floating crap game? As a few unfortunate gamblers hit each year for tax evasion can testify, the answer is yes: The IRS does have a man everywhere there is a big winner. The "man" is the establishment itself.

Nobody likes it very much, but the law makes the gambling establishment into an enforcement arm of the IRS. And the operator of an illegal game, who naturally enough will not report to the IRS when one of his players wins big, can find himself investigated by the FBI and subject to federal prosecution.

In a legal gaming establishment, a bingo or slot machine winner of over $1200 and a keno winner of over $1500 will be handed a Form W-2G "Statement of Certain Gambling Winnings" along with his winnings. The winner is required to present two types of identification to aid the casino in filling out the form. Since most winners are more than a little reluctant to tell the IRS about their big win, the casino is put into a sticky situation: The casino can either get into a fight with the big winner (bad for public relations) or get into a fight with the IRS (bad for staying out of jail). The Nevada Gaming Control Board recognized "This requirement poses a problem for management when the winning patron does not have or refuses to produce the required two pieces of identification. While the Gaming Control Board does not wish to be the primary means of enforcing the Federal regulations, the Board does feel compelled to assist the gaming licensee (casino) with the identification problem." The Board wisely set up a twenty-four hour, seven days-a-week phone number to its Enforcement Division to assist the casinos in dealing with uncooperative winners.

Other big winners were specifically covered by the Internal Revenue Code and Regulations of the IRS, and to add injury to insult, the law provides for withholding by the gambling establishment before winnings are paid. A lottery winner of over $5,000 will find the state withholds 20 percent for federal taxes. Jai alai, horse, and dog racing also have 20 percent withholding on winnings if the amount won is over $1,000 and is also at least 300 times the amount bet.

Tournament winners are specifically covered by Form 1099 Misc, which requires businesses to report prizes and awards given to non-employees if over $600.

In fact, all gambling winnings are subject to a catchall "$600 or more" rule in the Internal Revenue Code: every person engaged in a trade of business who pays $600 or more to another person in any taxable year is required to file an information return with the IRS. The law has not been generally applied to casinos, but could be.

The most skillful players of poker and blackjack thus have an interesting test of their game-playing ability: how to factor in the IRS? The penalties for failure to report winnings can be very severe, yet, the chances of getting caught are slight if the player sticks to illegal games. However, the chances of being cheated should more than off-set any possible tax gain, particularly if the game is run by an underground casino.

In sticking with legal games, should the player enter a tournament? The IRS has done virtually nothing to go after winners in regular games. When a player cashes in $5,000 worth of chips, the card room or casino has no way of knowing whether he bought in for $100 or $1000. However, the taxman has gone after tournament winners, where the house knows exactly how much the winners of the big prizes have made.

So far, most skilled players have preferred to share their prizes with the IRS rather then give up the chance for big money, fame, and the satisfaction of showing the world they are the best. But, I suspect, at least one or two professional poker players have failed to make the final round on purpose; figuring they can make more from the side action, without having to tip off the IRS that they (the side bets) even exist.

17

◆

Sweepstakes and Taxes: Paying the Piper, A.K.A. Uncle Sam

by Tom Stamatson

PART ONE: TAX ISSUE OVERVIEW

You have been a winner! Congratulations—but now you have to tackle the issue of your tax liability.

By now, you should have received all your 1099 forms from sponsors that awarded you prizes. You must report any and all income, and this includes sweepstakes and gambling winnings.

Get your forms via fax at 703-368-9694.

Any and all winnings are considered Miscellaneous Income. Among these are:

Free Trip: A free trip or tour you receive from a travel agency for organizing a group of tourists must be included as income at the fair market value of the tour. FAIR MARKET VALUE is the price at which the travel agency sells the trip to the other members of the group. This would also extend to winning a trip in a sweepstakes or contest.

Lottery Winnings: You must include your gambling winnings as income. If you itemize your deductions on Form 1040, Schedule A, you may deduct gambling losses you had UP TO the amount of your winnings.

FAIR MARKET VALUE is the price at which the property would change hands between the buyer and a seller, neither being required to buy or sell, and both having reasonable knowledge of all necessary facts. If you win a state-lottery prize payable in installments, you must include as income both the annual payments and any amount designated as "interest" on the unpaid installments. Any federal income tax withheld from your gambling winnings should be included on your return. Be sure to attach your Form W-2G to your return.

Sweepstakes Winnings: If you win any prize, you must include its fair market value as income.

And don't forget the state taxes—are you getting a headache yet?

PART TWO: 1099 MISCELLANEOUS INCOME

Miscellaneous Income is defined as:

Gambling winnings: You must include your gambling winnings in your income on line 21 of Form 1040. If you itemize your deductions on Schedule A (Form 1040), you can deduct gambling losses you had during the year, but only up to the amount of your winnings.

Lotteries and raffles: Winnings from lotteries and raffles are gambling winnings. In addition to cash winnings, you must include in your income the fair market value of bonds, cars, houses, and other noncash prizes.

Installment Payments: Generally, if you win a state lottery prize payable in installments, you must include in your gross income the annual payments and any amounts you receive designated as "interest" on the unpaid installments. If you sell future lottery payments for a lump sum, you must report the amount you receive from the sale as ordinary income (line 21, Form 1040) in the year you receive it.

Form W-2G: You may have received a Form W-2G, Certain Gambling Winnings, showing the amount of your gambling winnings and any taxes taken out of them. Include the amount from box 1 on line 21 of Form 1040. Be sure to include any amount from box 2 on line 58 of Form 1040.

Illegal Income: Illegal income, such as stolen or embezzled funds, must be included in your gross income on line 21 of Form 1040, or on Schedule C or Schedule C-EZ (Form 1040) if from your self-employment activity. (Yes, this is a laugh!)

Prizes and awards: If you win a prize in a lucky-number drawing, television, or radio quiz program, beauty contest, or other event, you must include it in your income. For example, if you win a $50 prize in a photography contest, you must report this income on line 21 of Form 1040. If you refuse to accept a prize, do not include its value in your income. Prizes and awards in goods or services must be included in your income at their fair market value.

Prizes: Scholarship prizes won in a contest are not scholarships or fellowships if you do not have to use the prizes for educational purposes. You must include these amounts in your gross income on line 21 of Form 1040, whether or not you use the amounts for educational purposes.

Check with your accountant as to deductions allowed. For example, if you had a substantial amount of income from online activities, you may be able to deduct your computer and Internet connection costs as well as your workspace within the home.

18

◆

Big Brother (the IRS) Is Watching

by Professor I. Nelson Rose

The Internal Revenue Code is unkind to winners—and it doesn't like losers, either. The federal government taxes gambling winnings at the highest rates allowed. So do the many states and even cities that impose income taxes on their residents. If you make enough money in a high-tax state like California or New York, the top tax bracket is about 50 percent. Out of every additional dollar you take in, through work or play, governments take fifty cents.

Of course, the tax collector first has to find out that you have won. Congress and the Internal Revenue Service know gambling is an all-cash business and few winners indeed would voluntarily report their good luck. So, statutes and regulations turn the gambling businesses, casinos, state lotteries, racetracks, and even bingo halls, into agents for the IRS.

Big winners are reported to the IRS on a special Form W-2G. If winnings are to be split, as with a lottery pool, winners are reported on a Form 5754.

Pooling money to buy lottery tickets is common among employees and friends. But whether there are two or two hundred in the pool, there is going to be only one winning ticket (for the pool of players), and somebody has to turn it in. If you are that someone, make sure

97

you fill out a Form 5754. If your share of a $5 million prize is $1 million, you do not want to be stuck with paying income tax on the entire $5 million.

Gambling has become such big business that the IRS receives nearly four million forms W-2G and 5754 each year. This tells the tax collectors that nearly four million big winners are out there, waiting to be taxed.

But the IRS does not always wait. The government wants to make sure it gets paid. What good does a W-2G do if the winner is a foreigner who is going to be in his own country when April 15 rolls around?

So, the IRS not only wants reports filed, but often requires that a part of the winnings be withheld. As anyone who has a salary knows, withholding also allows the government to use taxpayers' money for many months, without having to pay interest.

The withholding rate for nonresident aliens is 30 percent. Not coincidentally, the tax rate for nonresident aliens is also 30 percent. So, if a citizen of a foreign country wins $1 million cash at a slot machine in Las Vegas, he will find he is only paid $700,000. The remaining $300,000 is sent to the IRS. The foreign citizen is unlikely to ever file an income tax return, but the IRS gets paid in full anyway.

Citizens of foreign countries are also, of course, taxed by their own governments. So some countries have treaties with the U.S. that protect those foreigners from having to pay the 30 percent withholding to the IRS.

U.S. citizens and resident aliens have it both better and worse than nonresident aliens. The withholding rate for gamblers living in America is only 28 percent (it was 20 percent up to 1992). Having the IRS take $28,000 of a jackpot of $100,000 is painful. But, it can hurt even more when the tax forms are filled out. There is no 30 percent maximum tax for people living in the U.S., and really big winners often end up paying a lot more than 28 percent or 30 percent.

The one good news is Nevada casinos were also able to convince the IRS that they could not keep track of players at table games. They said that when a player cashes out for $7,000 they do not know whether they started with $25 or $25,000. So it is actually written into the law that there is no withholding or even reporting of big winnings to the IRS for blackjack, baccarat, craps, roulette, or the big-6 wheel.

There is another general IRS rule that says anyone paying anyone else $600 in one year is supposed to file a report. The IRS has been going after casinos and card rooms that run tournaments, forcing them to file tax-reporting forms on grand-prize winners. Here, the IRS has the very good argument that the operator knows exactly how much a player has paid to enter the tournament and how much finalists are given.

Is there anything a winning player can do to lower the bite of the income tax? And what about those who gamble and lose? Which is everybody, occasionally. The law does allow players to take gambling losses off of their taxes, but only up to the amounts of their winnings.

Of course, if you win, say $135,000, you can take off all gambling losses up to that amount. If you gambled away, say $65,000, you would only have to pay taxes on the remaining, let's see: $135,000 minus $65,000 equals $70,000. The tax on $70,000 is a lot less than the tax on $135,000.

Of course, you have the small problem of proving that you actually lost $65,000. Large winnings may be required to be reported to the IRS; large losses are not.

One former IRS revenue officer, who quit government to open his own small tax-preparation firm, thought he had found the answer. One of his clients won a share in a state lottery: $2.7 million, paid out over twenty years in installments of about $135,000, before taxes. The winnings were reported, but the tax return claimed gambling losses of $65,000. The IRS decided that $65,000 was a lot to lose, and it sent an agent to conduct an audit.

The tax preparer found a man with an extremely large collection of losing lottery tickets and made a deal: he would borrow 200,000 losing tickets for a month for $500. The losing tickets were bound in stacks of one hundred and shown to the IRS auditor: 45,000 instant scratch tickets, 5,000 other Massachusetts lottery tickets, and 16,000 losing tickets from racetracks throughout New England. So many losing tickets, that it would have been physically impossible for one man to have made these bets. *The New York Times* called it, "one of the more visibly inept efforts at tax fraud." They (the tax preparer and his client) pleaded guilty eight days after being indicted.

By the way, the man who rented the tickets was not charged. It's not a crime to collect losing lottery tickets, only to use them to try to cheat the IRS.

RULES FOR TAX REPORTS AND WITHHOLDINGS ON WINNINGS

1. Slot machines and bingo—payouts of $1,200 or more are reported to the IRS, but there is no withholding taken out.
2. Keno—similar to slot machines, but the amount won must be at least $1,500.
3. State lotteries and sweepstakes—withholding is taken out of all winnings of more than $5,000.
4. Pari-mutuel pools, including horse and dog races—subject to withholding, but only if the winnings are both more than $5,000 and at least 300 times as large as the amount bet.

19

Bet on It: The IRS Doesn't Get Its Cut of Gambling Winnings

by Kay Bell, Bankrate.com

Picked the Super Bowl winner yet? As the game nears, millions of Americans are choosing, and betting on, their favorite to take home the Vince Lombardi Trophy this year.

Many are just friendly wagers—a dollar in the office pool, a good-natured bet with the neighbor who seems to live in that Rams jersey.

But just as many football fans are taking the game more seriously and handing over big bucks to bookmakers, both legal and not so legal. All these Super Bowl wagers spotlight a persistent Internal Revenue Service problem: tracking and taxing gambling winnings.

It's a challenge the agency faces daily because many people don't realize that gambling winnings are taxable. Of those who do, a good portion simply choose to ignore the law.

AMERICA'S REAL PASTIME

Gambling has been around at least since man was able to record his activities. Dice almost identical to those used on today's gaming tables have been recovered from Egyptian tombs and Chinese excavations dating to 600 B.C.

In addition to the offerings of Las Vegas and Atlantic City, betting is commonplace throughout the United States. The choices range from off-track betting parlors to charitable bingo games to riverboat casinos to state-operated lotteries.

Then there are the online gambling opportunities. A check of any Internet search engine will turn up thousands of sites. Here you can place a bet by credit card or other electronic payment method, although some card issuers are denying gambling-related transactions, citing risk factors if the cardholder disputes or refuses to pay the charges. These Web sites typically are foreign headquartered to avoid running afoul of U.S. and state laws against the practice.

Couple all these gambling options with Americans' love of athletics, and betting on sporting events has arguably become the true national pastime.

SO MANY EVENTS, SO MANY BETS

In the United States, legal betting on sports is allowed only in Nevada, and Las Vegas draws millions of visitors each year expressly for that purpose. Casino operators there report more than $2 billion is bet annually on athletic events, including racing and professional collegiate sports.

The annual Super Bowl weekend is one of the biggest in the gaming industry, with a record $77.3 million bet in Nevada on the 1998 game (Denver beat Green Bay). For the last few years, the amounts have hovered around the $70 million range.

The dollars add up because there are countless ways to get a piece of the action. Wagers aren't just placed on the eventual winner. You can bet on who will catch the first pass, who will rush for the most yardage (team and individual), or who will get the first sack.

If it happens in a football game, the sports book operation will take a bet on it.

But casino bets aren't a real concern for the IRS. The tax man has a way to track those dollars. It's a dicier tax proposition when it comes to the millions bet at increasingly popular offshore sports-betting operations, illegal wagers placed with bookies, and all those friendly office pools.

WHY THE BELLS GO OFF

Legal betting operations—state lotteries, casinos and horse racing tracks—are regulated. One of the government agencies that has a say in these operations is the IRS.

When a patron hits the long-shot trifecta, picks the six lucky lotto numbers, or lines up all the cherries on the slot machine, the establishment paying off the bet makes sure that it gets the gambler's vital tax information. If your winnings are more than $5,000, Uncle Sam generally gets his cut in withholding before you get your payout.

"That's why the bells go off when you hit the slots," says John Shelk of the American Gaming Association. "So we can get someone there to get your tax information."

Come next tax-filing time, the casino will send you—and the IRS—a Form W-2G showing how much you won and how much was withheld for federal taxes. But, Shelk notes, there's a distinction between what's reportable and what's taxable.

All gambling winnings—regardless of the amount—are taxable. But it's ultimately the winner's responsibility to let the IRS know how much was won, even if the casino doesn't have to file a W-2G. This reliance on the gambler's tax-law compliance is where the IRS frequently gets shortchanged.

How tempting is it to assume the IRS won't miss a small jackpot? Apparently pretty darn appealing.

"On a trip to Vegas, I won $146 on a slot machine," admits a chagrined economics professor at a church-financed university, "and I didn't report it on my tax return."

MAKING A BAD DAY AT THE TRACK PAY OFF

The professor's tax reporting inclination is one shared by many gaming winners, but not all.

IRS analysis of 1999 returns, the latest year for which data is completed, shows more than 1.4 million taxpayers did report gambling income of more than $15 billion. This includes winnings from casinos and horse tracks, lottery and raffle jackpots, as well as the fair market value of cars, houses, and other noncash prizes.

As for how many taxpayers didn't bare all about their betting at tax time, the IRS won't even venture a guess. "We can't tell you what we don't know," says Don Roberts at IRS headquarters in Washington, D.C.

But the IRS has a tax break for those conscientious taxpayers who report their gambling income on line 21 of their Form 1040. Tax law allows you to subtract any gambling losses from your winnings if you itemize. For many, that's a good deal. Gamblers in 1999 made their good luck less taxing by claiming almost $8 billion in bad bets.

Losses to reduce gambling winnings don't have to be from the same game. If you go to the race track every weekend and drop $1,000, but then win $3,000 on the World Series, those losing horse-betting slips can reduce the amount of baseball winnings that you'll be taxed on.

There are a couple of ground rules to keep in mind here. First, you can't claim more in losses than you won. And, as with any tax deduction, you need to keep records of your losses that will satisfy the IRS if you're ever audited.

GOOD RECORDS ARE THE BEST BET

Roberts recommends keeping track of gambling losses as you go through the year so you're not scrambling to reconstruct them if you do hit it big.

Such reconstruction efforts not only are difficult, they aren't likely to pass IRS scrutiny. Tax professionals recall a horse-race fanatic who went to tax court with bags full of losing betting slips to support his large deduction against his winnings.

It didn't work; almost every ticket was covered with the footsteps of other bettors who tossed the tickets when their horses didn't win. He ended up paying the extra tax—and penalties.

"It's not a tax myth, but it is an old story," Roberts said, who saw similar actions when he was an agent in Saratoga, New York, early in his tax career.

"And if you don't have a big win to offset," he adds, "then the receipts can be your ticket to Gamblers Anonymous."

20

◆

Supreme Court Gives Tax Break to Professional Gamblers

by Professor I. Nelson Rose

The Supreme Court of the United States recently decided what may be the most important decision ever for professional gamblers. The high court ended decades of indecision by declaring that professional gamblers may be considered as being in a trade or business for tax purposes, just like any other business.

The case is titled *Commissioner of Internal Revenue* v. *Groetzinger*, and involved a taxpayer who devoted sixty to eighty hours per week studying and betting on dog races. The Court rejected the arguments of the Internal Revenue Service and the decisions of some lesser courts that would have required the bettor to take bets, like a bookie, before he could claim to be in a trade or business. Instead, the justices said that each case must be examined on its own facts to determine the tax status for the bettor.

As Justice Blackmun put it, writing for a six to three majority:

> If a taxpayer, as Groetzinger is stipulated to have done in 1978, devotes his full-time activity to gambling, and it is his intended livelihood source, it would seem that basic concepts of fairness (if there be much of that in the income tax law) demand that his activity be regarded as a trade or business just

as any other readily accepted activity, such as being a retail store proprietor or, to come closer categorically, as being a casino operator or as being an active trader on the exchanges.

The implications of this decision are great, for taxes, and possibly for other areas of the law. This is the first time the Supreme Court has acknowledged that legal gambling not only exists, but that there are individuals who work very hard at making legitimate wagers. Legal gambling remains a suspect enterprise, but at least the Court now recognizes that it can be a legitimate business, from both sides of the tables.

Even if the decision is limited to tax law, it can have an enormous impact on a gambler's taxes. The dissent tried to say that the decision is limited to the old tax code, but as the quote above shows, the Court is clearly holding that a full-time job of gambling qualifies the gambler for treatment as a businessman. What this means for the gambler is literally worth hundreds or thousands of dollars.

The tax code definitely discriminates against the gambler, as opposed to, say, the stock speculator. A gambler can only take his gambling losses off up to the amount of his winnings. Each year is treated separately so a big loss in 1996 cannot be carried over to offset a big win in 1997. Expenses incurred in gambling are not deductible at all. And gamblers cannot take advantage of other tax breaks given legitimate businesses.

Until now.

After the Groetzinger decision it is only the casual gambler who faces this discrimination. A full-time gambler can now have all of the tax advantages available to all other working taxpayers. Expenses incurred in gambling can now be deducted, losses are no longer limited to the amount of winnings, and losses and expenses should be available to be carried forward to offset winnings in future years, or even be carried backward by amending tax filings for past years.

Robert P. Groetzinger himself was the first beneficiary of this new treatment for professional gamblers. Groetzinger lost his job in February 1978 and spent the rest of the year at the dog tracks. The court ruled that he did not have to pay a minimum tax on his $70,000 winnings because he had $72,032 in losses. You don't even have to be a winner to be ruled a professional gambler—Groetzinger lost $2,032 in the year the Supreme Court ruled him to be in the trade, or business, of gambling.

If you are a full-time gambler, the Groetzinger decision is a powerful tool because it gives you a choice. For most gamblers, it would probably pay to declare yourself in the trade or business. You could even take expenses off, such as all of your travel, meals, and hotel bills, etc., as well as the cost of this magazine and my book *Gambling and the Law*, which contains more gambling tax information. You could set up a Keogh retirement account and deduct those contributions from your taxes.

On the other hand, declaring yourself a professional gambler might subject you to self-employment taxes. But if being in the trade or business of gambling would result in more rather than less taxes, simply go out of "business" and remain a casual gambler.

To get the new tax breaks you must devote full-time to your business, which I interpret to be at least 6–8 hours a day. Card counters, poker players, handicappers, and "prop" players should qualify. Although the Groetzinger case involved a gambler with no other job, I don't think that is a requirement. However, it is not for the casual bettor. As the court put it:

> We accept the fact that to be engaged in a trade or business, the taxpayer must be involved in the activity with continuity and regularity and that the taxpayer's primary purpose for engaging in the activity must be for income or profit. A sporadic activity, a hobby, or an amusement diversion does not qualify.

In addition, you must keep detailed, accurate records and receipts. Remember, this isn't just a game—you're now a professional.

21

◆

Ask the Gambling Expert

by Basil Nestor, author of
The Unofficial Guide to Casino Gambling

Q: This sounds strange, but I think I may have been robbed. I'm not quite sure because it happened at a craps table during a hot streak. Everyone was shouting. I was winning a mountain of chips. I thought I had about $2,000 sitting on the rail, and then it was suddenly more like $1,500. Nobody acted suspicious, and I couldn't be absolutely sure, so I said nothing. I left the table about thirty minutes later, and I've been scratching my head ever since. What do you think?

A: Yes, you were probably robbed. It's unfortunate, but the mixture of money, confusing noises, tourists in "fun mode," and the constant push of the crowd in a casino creates a prime environment for larceny. Purses, wallets, bags, cups of coins, chips, and anything not nailed down or attached to one's body are in danger of disappearing into a mass of pulsing humanity.

In fact, personal security and handling money are such important gaming issues that I devoted two entire chapters to those subjects in *The Unofficial Guide to Casino Gambling.* Below are some personal-safety tips that apply in Las Vegas, Atlantic City, or anywhere else you may find a casino.

1. Avoid carrying a purse or bag. If a bag must be carried, it should be placed between your legs or in your lap when sitting.

2. Thieves often use a loud noise or a nearby disturbance to distract attention while they grab unattended chips, coins, or bags. If you hear a loud noise, or you see a disturbance, look down and secure your belongings BEFORE you look up to see what is happening.

3. If someone "accidentally" bumps into you hard enough to knock you off balance, don't worry about who will apologize to whom. Immediately assume you are being robbed. Tightly hold on to anything you want to keep because in the next millisecond it will be forcibly torn from your hand, arm, or pocket. Also, beware when you're "accidentally" doused with a spilled drink. The loud ditzy blonde who is frenetically dabbing your gin-soaked crotch may be covering for a confederate who is scooping up your chips.

4. Don't toddle upstairs with twenty black chips stuffed into your pocket. Cash out and leave most of it on deposit at the "cage." That's the banklike area of the casino, where money transactions are conducted.

5. If you MUST carry a large amount of cash, ask the casino for a security escort. Don't be embarrassed. That's casino security's job. Do it even if you're a tough guy. Anyone can be robbed.

6. Don't expect a casino's high-tech wonder toys to help much when someone has stolen your money. Surveillance systems are primarily designed to detect cheating rather than rectify patron-on-patron theft. And the "eye-in-the-sky" only works when a casino can stop criminals in the act. There's not much that can be done AFTER the crime, when the criminal has disappeared. Craps players should be especially diligent because a hot table usually involves a lot of shouting and a throng of people who are elbow to elbow. It's a good idea to keep an eye (or a hand) on your chips to prevent any light-fingered larceny.

22

◆

How to Double Casinos' Jackpots for Free

by Professor I. Nelson Rose

A minor change in the federal tax laws should allow casinos to double the size of their advertised jackpots without having to pay an additional cent.

State lotteries have known, and used, this marketing tool for decades. But, only a few of the very biggest casino jackpots have been advertised this way.

The trick? Advertise that you are offering a prize of, say, $1 million—but pay it out at the rate of $50,000 a year for twenty years.

Twenty payments of $50,000 equals $1 million, right?

Anyone with a mortgage understands there is something wrong with this picture. Imagine borrowing the million dollars from a bank to buy a house, and being able to pay it back in exactly twenty payments of $50,000 each.

The problem is that a payment of $50,000 in the year 2019 is not worth $50,000 today. You can call it "present value of money," or just plain "nobody lends you that kind of money without charging interest."

Interest rates (also called the discount rate) vary. But, it is safe to say that in today's market, a prize paid out over twenty years is only worth about half the total. You can buy an annuity from an insurance company that will pay out $1 million over the next twenty years for about $500,000.

State lotteries have been accused of misleading advertising for promoting these large, annuitylike jackpots; but they have won every challenge. Lottery ads always clearly indicate that prizes over a certain amount will be paid out over time.

Most players do not want their jackpots paid out like an annuity. They want a lump sum, which they can spend today.

State lotteries and legislatures were reluctant to let players get their winnings all at once. Lottery officials knew that many players would quickly blow everything, leaving them without enough money to pay their large tax bills the following April 15.

Under federal tax law, as it existed up until October 1998, lotteries had to be extremely careful about offering winners any choice in how the prize was paid.

Tax law had developed the "constructive receipt" rule: You have to pay income tax this year on money that has been put aside for you, money that you can collect whenever you want, even if you put off being paid until next year.

Winners given the option of receiving a lump sum or an annuity had to pay taxes on the lump sum, even if they chose payments over time.

Congress changed the tax law as part of the appropriations bill for 1999. Their motive was not to help players, but to raise money for Medicare.

During one of the last budget crises, Congress and the president worked out a deal: No new spending program would be approved unless funding could be found for it, without raising taxes. So, when Congress wanted to increase Medicare benefits, it had to find "revenue offsets."

Someone came up with the idea of allowing lottery winners who collect over time to pay their taxes in the years they actually receive their payments, even if they had had the option of receiving a lump sum.

I cannot quite figure out how this is supposed to increase tax revenue. Maybe some winners who choose annuities, but who were then taxed as if they had received a lump sum, were unable to pay their large bills. Under the new law, the IRS will be able to collect in full for the entire life of the annuity.

For casinos, the new tax law opens a golden opportunity. The statute has only a few requirements, which are easy to meet:

1. The winner must be given the option of receiving a lump sum or a "qualified prize";
2. The winner has to decide within sixty days of becoming entitled to the prize;
3. A "qualified prize" is a jackpot that is payable over a period of at least ten years.

If all requirements are met, the winner who chooses the "qualified prize" only pays income taxes as the payments are actually received.

Casinos would now be justified in advertising all of their large jackpots paid out over ten years as the total amount of all payments, not the much smaller present-day cash value.

Only after a player has won will he or she be told that they have the option of taking the present-day cash value in one lump sum. The overwhelming majority will undoubtedly want the lump sum. But, the game is still technically an annuity game and can be advertised with the much larger payout.

Naturally, players must also be told that these large prizes will be paid over ten or twenty years. The law also requires payers to disclose how they computed the value of the single-cash payment. Players must be told that they are under no obligation to accept the lump sum.

Casinos should have their lawyers check out local state laws to ensure that annuity jackpots are legal. There should be little trouble having gaming regulations changed to match the federal tax laws. But, care must also be taken that the state income tax laws are updated to get rid of the constructive receipt rule for these prizes.

Of course, Nevada casinos do not have to worry about whether their state income tax laws coincide with the new federal tax law. It is just one more advantage of being in a state without a state income tax.

23

◆

Hit the Big One? Here's How to Report the Winnings and Deduct the Losses

by Kay Bell, Bankrate.com

Lady Luck must be Uncle Sam's cousin because taxes have to be paid on all gambling winnings.

If you just hit the big one, here's a look at the federal tax forms you'll need and how to fill them out to share your good fortune with the Internal Revenue Service. And if you lost a few rounds before your numbers came up, there's a way you can turn those losses to your tax advantage.

The requirements for the reporting of and withholding from a winning wager depend on the type of gambling, the amount won, and the ratio of the winnings to the wager. When you pocket $600 or more (or 300 times your bet) at a horse track, win $1,200 at bingo or a slot machine, or take $1,500 or more from a keno game, the payer must get your Social Security number and let the IRS know that you came into the extra income.

And if you're lucky enough to rake in $5,000 or more on a gambling transaction, you're probably not going to walk away with all the cash you won. In this case, in addition to telling Uncle Sam that you were a winner and for how much, the payer in most cases must reduce your payout by withholding federal taxes at the 27 percent rate. If you try to shortchange the IRS by refusing to furnish your Social

Security number, the payer could take as much at 30 percent of your winnings right off the top to send to the tax collector.

In either instance, you'll get a Form W-2G showing the amount you won and, if applicable, how much in taxes you paid on it upfront.

WHEN YOU HAVE TO REPORT IT

Even if you didn't win enough to trigger a W-2G filing, you do want to be a diligent taxpayer and report those gambling winnings, right? Just because the casino or track or lottery agent didn't report that $25 dollars you won doesn't mean it's not taxable. It's ultimately the taxpayer's responsibility to tell Uncle Sam about his good fortune.

You report your winnings—from the W-2G or those smaller jackpots—on line 21, Other Income, of Form 1040. In addition to gambling proceeds, this is where you'd also report any prizes or awards (cash or cash value) you won. All this money goes toward your adjusted gross-income amount.

You don't have to pay taxes on all that AGI, however. You can reduce it through claiming deductions, either the standard amount or by itemized deductions. When deciding to itemize, you should compare to see if it would provide you a bigger deduction than claiming the standard one.

If you have large gambling winnings and losses, itemizing may be preferable. In this case, enter your gambling losses on line 27, Other Miscellaneous Deductions, of Schedule A.

It's also a good idea to keep a record of the gambling losses you're deducting. While you don't have to send it as part of your return, documentation could come in handy if the IRS ever questions your losses. Acceptable gambling loss record keeping could include a written log detailing the date of your wagers, the location, amount bet, type of gaming, and wins and losses. You should also hang on to losing lottery tickets or bingo cards.

The good thing about deducting gambling losses is that, unlike some other deductions, you don't have to meet a certain level before you can claim them. But then again, they aren't completely unlimited.

You can only count as much in losses as you won. So if you spent $100 on lottery tickets and won $75, you can only deduct $75. The other $25 is just part of the price of playing the game.

24

◆

Casinos As Spies for the Federal Government

by Professor I. Nelson Rose

The following Notice has not been approved by any government official. (In fact, some of them would probably be unhappy to see this warning published.)

WARNING TO ALL CASINO PATRONS

If you win big, are a high roller, or do anything that a casino or the government regards as suspicious, you will be reported to the U.S. Treasury Department's Financial Crimes Enforcement Network, commonly known as FinCEN. The information will be made available to the IRS and your local law-enforcement agency. Expect your taxes to be audited. If you are ever involved in a messy lawsuit, your opponent may be able to obtain some of this information by subpoena, to show, for example, how much cash you used for gambling. The casino will not always tell you when it files these reports; in fact, under some circumstances, it is not allowed to let you know that you have been reported to FinCEN.

Scary, isn't it?

All businesses are supposed to report cash transactions over $10,000. But only "financial institutions" are required to file detailed

reports and have compliance programs in place to make sure the reports get filed. And only "financial institutions" have to report "suspicious activities" involving more than $3,000 to FinCEN.

It may come as a surprise to most players and even executives in
the gaming industry that large casinos and card clubs have been defined as "financial institutions."

It will certainly be a shock to most players to learn that they may
be the subject of secret reports filed by casinos with the federal government.

All casinos and card clubs with gross, annual gaming revenues in
excess of $1 million must file Currency Transaction Reports (CTRs)
with the federal government every time a player has a cash transaction of $10,000. This includes players using currency to buy chips,
deposit front money, pay off markers, make large wagers, or collect
large winning bets.

The last is particularly interesting, because the original purpose of
CTRs was to track crooks who were using casinos for money laundering, like a drug dealer who bought gaming chips with $25,000 in
small bills, made a few token bets, and then asked for a cashier's
check for his remaining chips.

In the mid-1980s, Nevada officials, including its then powerful Re-
publican senators, convinced the federal government that there was no
need for casinos to file CTRs when the cash was paid by casinos themselves. Nevada enacted Regulation 6A, which required casinos to file
CTRs only with the state, and only for transactions that might conceiv-
ably involve dirty money, like cash buy-ins or marker payments.

But Nevada gaming officials, apparently at the request of the federal government, changed the rules in 1997. All currency transactions
of more than $10,000, even slot jackpots paid out in cash, now have to
be reported. And today CTRs are filed with the IRS, not with the state.

The U.S. Congress, which is supposedly the body that actually
makes the laws, had established complicated rules for withholding
taxes of gambling winnings, but only under special circumstances.
For example, a sports book has to withhold 28 percent of the amount
won, but only if it is more than $5,000 and at least 300 times as large
as the amount bet.

For years the IRS has gone further by requiring casinos to report big wins at bingo, slot machines, and keno, even though no money was withheld for taxes.

Today, a CTR must be filed on every patron who cashed out for more than $10,000 in currency—no matter what the game and even if the player has lost money gambling.

The regulations also used to require that casinos obtain identification from the player before filing a CTR.

Today, a casino does not have to ask for a player's ID if it already has the patron's name, address, and similar information. This eases the casinos' workload and prevents disruptions. But it also means high rollers do not have to be told when the casino files CTRs with the IRS.

The reason for the changes is simple: The Treasury Department has admitted that one of its primary goals is to go after untaxed cash transactions that have nothing to do with money laundering.

But, Treasury still wants to catch drug dealers. So, it has taken the next step: "Suspicious Activity Reports—Casinos" or SARCs, to be filed with FinCEN.

As this is being written, only Nevada casinos have to file SARCs, although FinCEN intends to require all casinos and card clubs to report suspicious activities.

What exactly is a "suspicious activity"?

The amount does not have to be more than $10,000; a total of $3,000 or less can trigger a report. Nor does it have to involve any currency.

FinCEN likes to say the standard is "know your patron." But the actual regulation is more vague, including phrases like a casino employee "has reason to suspect" that the transaction "has no business or apparent lawful purpose."

Casinos face large fines if they fail to report suspicious transactions, and they cannot be sued for filing SARCs when players were doing nothing wrong. So, when in doubt, casinos will err on the side of filing reports on their patrons.

It is against the law for a casino to tell a player that it has reported his suspicious activity to FinCEN.

This might catch more crooks. But it is hard to picture casino executives as secret police.

25

◆

If I Win Money Gambling, Do I Have to Pay Taxes on It?

by James W. Crawford, CPA

Many people wonder how gambling activities are treated for tax purposes. Taxpayers often run into tax difficulties in this area. This is because gambling winnings are fully taxable, while gambling losses aren't simply offset against the winnings. Briefly, your winnings must be reported on "other income" line 21 on the front page of your tax return. To measure your winnings on a particular wager, just use the net gain on the wager. For example, if a $20 bet at the racetrack turns into a $100 win, you have won just $80, not $100. If you lose $50 on a different race, however, you cannot simply offset this amount against your $80 win.

You must separately keep track of losses. They are deductible, but only as itemized deductions (on line 27 of Schedule A of your Form 1040). Thus, if you take the standard deduction (i.e., don't itemize), you cannot deduct your gambling losses. On the other hand, if you do itemize, the gambling losses fall into the category of "Other miscellaneous deductions." These are fully deductible as itemized deductions and aren't subject to either the 2 percent of adjusted gross income (AGI) floor, or the 3 percent/80 percent phase out of certain itemized deductions. (Some types of miscellaneous itemized deductions, such as investment expenses and unreimbursed employee expenses are only deductible to the extent they exceed, in total, 2 percent of AGI. And if a taxpayer's AGI exceeds a specified dollar amount, certain itemized deductions are reduced by the lesser of 3 percent of the excess AGI over that dollar amount, or 80 percent of the otherwise allowable itemized deductions.) A second important limitation is that your gambling losses are only deductible up to the amount of your gambling winnings. That is, for tax purposes, you can use your losses to "wipe out" your gambling income, but you can never show a gambling tax loss.

Be careful to keep good records of your losses during the year. Keep a diary in which you indicate the date, place, amount, and type of loss as well as the names of any people who were with you. Save all documentation, such as losing tickets, checks, or credit slips. You should also save any related "side" documentation, for example, if you have losses on a trip to Las Vegas, save the hotel bill and plane ticket, any receipts from cash machines in the casino, as well as your records on the gambling losses themselves. If you join a slot club, ask the casino if you can get a printout of the amount you bet. Since anyone can just pick up, e.g., an unlimited amount of losing tickets at a race track, the IRS may require more data and documentation to substantiate gambling-loss deductions.

26

◆

The Cruelest Tax

by Professor I. Nelson Rose

If you win big, really big, and then die suddenly, your family could end up paying more in taxes than your total prize.

The question I am asked most often is, "What happens if I win the lottery, and then die?"

It is too bad players limit this question to state lotteries. Other forms of gambling also pay out large prizes over time. Which is fine, if you live to collect all the payments.

Linked, progressive slot machine networks can be found in both Nevada and Atlantic City. The biggest is International Game Technology's Megabucks™, tying together 628 slot machines in 127 Nevada casinos. On May 30, 1992, Delores Adams, 59, a Sacramento nurse, put in $12 and lined up winning symbols for a Megabucks™ prize of $9.3 million. This world-record slot machine jackpot will be paid out in twenty annual installments of $467,000, before taxes.

Gamma International has tied together over sixty high-stakes bingo halls, mostly on Indian land, into the largest sustained bingo game in history. Megabingo™ regularly pays out millions of dollars in jackpots. These prizes, too, are paid out in annual installments.

Paying in installments was originally designed by the state lotteries to protect big winners from blowing their winnings, and to help with the then-progressive federal income tax. It also allows operators to announce a "$10 million jackpot," which only costs them about $5 million to fund, in today's dollars.

First, the good news.

Even if you die, the prizes will continue to be paid to your estate.

Now, the bad news.

The following numbers are only approximations, but they will give you some idea of what can happen with death and taxes. They come from a letter written by the director of the Virginia Lottery, Kenneth W. Thorson, on behalf of the North American Association of State and Provincial Lotteries, to the U.S. Treasury Department in an attempt to get the federal government to change its tax policy.

Start with an average player, middle-class, who wins a $20 million jackpot, $1 million a year for twenty years. The first million is paid immediately, less federal and perhaps state income taxes withheld.

The big winner then dies, before the second year's payment of $1 million.

According to the IRS, the winner is leaving an estate worth about $9.5 million. This is the present-day value of those future payments of $1 million each for the next nineteen years.

The current tax rate on gross estates over $3 million is 55 percent. So the heirs owe $5.225 million. They have nine months to come up with the money.

The estate is in trouble. Under virtually every state law, future lottery-prize payments cannot be sold or used as collateral for a loan.

When the family cannot make the $5 + million tax payment, the IRS starts assessing penalties and interest. The monthly penalty is one-half percent, or $26,125 up to 25 percent, or a total of $1,306,250.

Interest accrues immediately, at 11 percent per year.

The tax bill is now growing at an average rate of more than $75,000 per month, for a total of over $900,000 by the end of the first year. This means the increase in the estate's taxes is greater each year than the amount the estate actually receives from the jackpot, after withholding. And there is still the little matter of the $5 + million already due in taxes.

The only way the "lucky" winner's heirs can avoid bankruptcy is to disclaim any interest in the prize.

Obviously, this situation is intolerable. But what can be done?

The immediate advice is for winners to get life insurance, enough to cover any estate tax. Of course, if you are ninety years old, the premium for life insurance could be greater than the first year's winnings.

In some states the estate might be able to get a court order allowing it to sell future payments, or at least use them for collateral for a loan to pay the estate taxes. But so far, most courts have not been friendly to the idea of allowing big winners to change their periodic payments into lump sums.

An estate could take the IRS to court. The IRS is relying on part of the tax code dealing with annuities. A court might understand that payments of big winnings over time only looks like an annuity; it isn't really, since the big winner had no choice in how the prize is to be paid.

The fastest, surest way to avoid this potential disaster is for Congress to change the law. Lottery and other gambling winnings paid out over time should be exempt from federal estate tax, or taxed at a lower rate due only as the prize is received.

The amount of tax money lost to the federal government would be insignificant. But the unnecessary suffering would be great.

The law should be changed, now, before a grieving family gets hurt.

27

◆

A. J.'s Tax Fables—Gambling

by A. J. Cook, CPA, attorney

PROVE GAMBLING LOSSES—BUT HOW?

With casinos nearby, more people are gambling. Many people, without realizing it, violate tax laws. They should be paying taxes on winnings, after reducing by losses—if you have proof of the losses.

Proof? How? You don't get receipts when playing the slots or blackjack.

Here are some cases.

Fred Schooler, of Scottsdale, Arizona, part owner of a carpet-laying business, was a part-time dog and horse race enthusiast. He didn't keep wagering records, nor did he report gains and losses on his tax return.

Unfortunately for Schooler, the Internal Revenue Service requires gambling facilities to report big winners. The agency had him down for $14,773 with no deductions.

The business executive said he didn't owe anything because his losses exceeded his winnings. As proof, he pointed out that he and his wife live modestly—in fact, they owed money.

The judge agreed with the IRS: A frugal lifestyle doesn't prove losses.

The Moral: Your winnings go to the dogs without records of lost bets.

James F. Klein fared a little better. The Texan traveled from Houston to Las Vegas. On his tax return he listed one trip with net winnings of $13,000, other trips with net losses of $10,000.

The IRS refused to deal him a winning hand. Because he had no records, it disallowed the deduction.

The judge, however, showed some compassion. Probably because Klein listed winnings exceeding the casino amount reported to the IRS, the judge allowed losses of $4,000—still far short of actual losses. He gently admonished Klein, saying he should have written down income and losses with trip dates, money taken on the trips, out-of-pocket expenses, and source of funds.

The Moral: The courts say no dice to deductions not backed with paper.

Leon Faulkner of Washington, D.C., often bet on horses. He thought he was only required to pay taxes on winnings the tracks reported to the IRS. To offset the underreporting, the agency arbitrarily disallowed his gaming deduction. The court allowed the losses after Faulkner supported them with his diary.

The Moral: Back your bets with pen and paper.

The Planning Tip: If you gamble, keep a diary or log. After each day write down the date, location, amount wagered, type of wager, net winnings or losses, and names of people accompanying you. If you can, support this with cancelled checks showing the money you took, expenses, and a bank deposit slip showing money remaining.

Even with all of this, you can't be sure the IRS won't challenge you. Regrettably, there is no ironclad formula as to adequacy of records.

Good Luck!

TAXING WINNINGS

Gary B. Bauman put four nickels into a progressive slot machine, and out poured $73,733. Accustomed to making $10,000 a year, this looked pretty good—until the Internal Revenue Service arrived.

Bauman, of Kingman, Arizona, had supported himself with his

nontaxable disability check and a small amount of interest income. After the big winnings, he started a spending binge: travel, furniture, a van, a mobile home. In a year and a half, he'd run through it all.

As was his custom, Bauman didn't file a tax return.

The IRS came calling for its share. The agency refused to accept his reason for not filing, so he went to court. He testified, "I always heard that, if you're on Social Security disability and you hit a jackpot . . . you didn't have to pay any income tax."

That didn't compute with the judge. "The taxpayer's argument is misguided," gambling winnings are always taxable. The judge ordered Bauman to pay the taxes plus penalties.

The Moral: Win, lose, or draw—pay, or the IRS can take it all.

A Nobel Prize isn't taxable, but an award for sales promotions is. And when it comes as a vacation, you pay on its market value.

But what is market value? Can you prove it?

Nathan L. Wade owned a Subaru car dealership in Salt Lake City. He advertised so much that over three years he won trips to Greece, Paris, Israel, Acapulco, and Monte Carlo. The prizes included transportation, hotels, and some meals.

The IRS challenged the amount he reported as income, so Wade appealed. Other recipients, he said, sold their awards for $2,000 each, so that's market value. But he presented no witnesses or other evidence.

In contrast, the IRS called representatives from award sponsors. They told the court exactly what the trips cost, much more than $2,000.

The judge accepted as Wade's income the figures given by the IRS witnesses.

The flaw here seems to have been the scarcity of evidence by Wade. In a similar case, but with witnesses for the taxpayer, the court accepted as market value the price other winners received from selling their awards.

The Moral: Sometimes it seems taxpayers can't win for losing.

Part III

USEFUL INFORMATION PUBLISHED BY THE INTERNAL REVENUE SERVICE

Glossary of Gambling Terms

Action
The amount of gaming activity happening in a casino, sporting event, or specific game.

Book
To accept wagers on the outcome of a sport or similarly uncertain event. (Race and sports book: the section in a casino where this type of bet is placed.)

Cage
Also called the "casino cage" or "cashier." A centralized enclosure where the records of transactions are kept and money is counted. Chips or tokens can be purchased or exchanged for cash.

Cage Credit
A condition allowing players to sign credit slips, or markers, for cash.

Card Rooms
Card rooms refer to gaming establishments where the principal activity is poker-related games, either live or video. These establishments typically do not offer slot-machine play or other table games such as blackjack, craps, or roulette. These establishments are governed and regulated by the state in which they are located.

Casino Gaming Industry
All of the activities related to legalized gambling and the operation of legal gambling establishments.

SOURCE: The Digital Daily; www.irs.gov/business/small. May 14, 2002.

Chip
Also known as "CHECK," and used to represent money. At one time, chips were made of ivory or bond, but now are made of composition, clay, ceramic, or plastic.

Coin Operated Gaming Device
Any mechanical or electronic machine designed to accept coins and to pay coins under certain conditions, especially a slot machine, pinball, video poker, or horse race machine.

Complimentary (also known as "comp")
A gift given by managers to favored patrons, such as meals, room, or show reservation.

Credit Line
Also shortened to "line." The amount of money a player has deposited into the casino cage, or the amount of money the casino manager is willing to advance to a player.

Drop
The amount wagered and lost at a table or machine.

Floating Casino
Taxpayers in the gaming industry include individuals, partners, corporations, and joint ventures operating gaming casinos on various facilities located in or near United States inland-river waterways, river basins, channels, lakes, ponds, and cofferdams. These operations are conducted under licenses issued by local and state gaming agencies. Often, state law prohibits gaming on land-based facilities and requires that the gaming facilities be on water. Operating casinos on the water are commonly referred to as "riverboat casinos". Operating casinos in water adjacent to land are commonly referred to as "dockside casinos." Taxpayers operating riverboat or dockside casinos conduct legalized gaming activities that include blackjack, poker, roulette, craps, baccarat, keno, and slot machines.

Gaming Activity
Involvement in gambling. The term is usually applied to legal gambling practices or involvement.

Gaming Commission
A state or city agency devoted to regulating legal gambling operations.

Gaming Control Act
A state statute that legalized certain forms of gambling and provides guidelines for the operation and taxation of gambling games.

Gaming Control Board
A state or county agency that enforces policies set by the gaming commission, investigates allegations of cheating, and provides background information on persons or corporations requesting licensing as operators of gambling establishments.

House
The casino.

Individual Taxpayer Identification Number (ITIN)
An Individual Taxpayer Identification Number is issued to nonresident aliens who do not have a Social Security number, and is used for tax purposes only.

Land-Based Casino
A land-based casino is one that is located on land and is owned either by individuals and/or corporations, which have their gambling operation overseen by a state gaming control board or state gaming commission. Some land-based casinos are limited by state law as to the maximum amount of a single wager or bet.

Lottery
A lottery is a game of chance based upon the random selection of numbers. Generally, lotteries are only legally operated by states, other governmental entities, or not-for-profit organizations.

Marker
Evidence of indebtedness by a player to the casino. A marker is usually a counter check. In craps, the term refers to a small rubber and plastic disk used to indicate whether a point has been made and to mark the number of the point until made or lost.

Pari-Mutuel

A system of betting on races, or events, whereby the winners divide the total amount bet, after deducting management expenses, in proportion to the sums they have wagered individually.

Pit

The area surrounded by a group of gaming tables.

Progressive Jackpot

In slot machines, a payout amount that increases with each coin played until the amount is won.

Racetracks

A racetrack (includes dog and horse racing, and jai alai) is one in which there is regular racetrack betting activity at a live racetrack and there may be video gambling machines located within the racing establishment premises. Racetracks are governed by the individual states.

Skim

To remove money from the profits before it is officially counted.

Slot Machine

A mechanical or electronic gaming device into which a player may deposit coins and from which certain numbers of coins are paid out when a particular configuration of symbols appear on the machine.

Tip

Also called a "toke." A sum of money given to a dealer, cocktail waitress, or other employee of an establishment for efficient or well-performed services.

Tribal Gaming

In 1988, Congress enacted the Indian Gaming Regulatory Act (IGRA) to:

1. Provide a statutory basis for the operation of gaming by Indian Tribes to promote tribal economic development, self-sufficiency, and strong tribal governments;
2. Provide a statutory basis for the regulation of Indian gaming to ensure the tribes are the primary beneficiaries;

3. Establish
   a. Independent Federal regulatory authority for Indian Gaming,
   b. Federal Standards for Indian Gaming, and
   c. The National Indian Gaming Commission (NIGC), to meet congressional concerns regarding Indian gaming and protect such gaming as a means of generating tribal revenue.

The term "gaming" has been divided by the IGRA into three classes: Class I gaming is defined as consisting of; (a) social games that have prizes of minimal value and (b) traditional tribal games planned in connection with tribal ceremonies or celebrations. Class II gaming primarily includes: bingo (whether or not it is electronically enhanced), pull tabs, lotto, punch boards, tip jars, instant bingo, and any nonbanking card games allowed by state law. Class III gaming primarily includes slot machines, casino games, banking card games, dog racing, horse racing, and lotteries.

All tribal governments conducting or sponsoring gaming activities need to be aware of the Federal requirements for Income Tax, Employment Tax, and Excise Tax. For further information, reference the IRS Indian Tribal Governments office Web site.

Wager
Something staked on an uncertain outcome.

Appendix I

◆

Gaming Activities by State

State	Land-Based Casinos	Card Rooms	Racetracks	Floating Casinos	Tribal Gaming	Lottery*
AL			●		●	
AK					●	
AZ			●		●	●
AR			●			
CA		●	●		●	●
CO	●		●		●	●
CT			●		●	●
DE			●			●
DC						●
FL			●		●	●
GA						●
HI						
ID			●		●	●
IL			●	●		●
IN			●	●		●
IA			●	●	●	●
KS			●		●	●
KY			●			●
LA	●		●	●	●	●
ME			●			●
MD			●			●
MA			●			●
MI	●		●		●	●
MN			●		●	●

*Additional lotteries: Multistate Lottery Association (Powerball), Puerto Rico, and Tri-State Lottery.

Source: The Digital Daily; www.irs.gov/business/small. May 14, 2002.

State	Land-Based Casinos	Card Rooms	Racetracks	Floating Casinos	Tribal Gaming	Lottery*
MS				●	●	
MO			●	●		●
MT		●	●		●	●
NE			●		●	●
NV	●		●		●	
NH			●			●
NJ	●		●			●
NM			●		●	●
NY			●		●	●
NC					●	
ND		●	●		●	
OH			●			●
OK			●		●	
OR			●		●	●
PA			●			●
RI			●			●
SC					●	●
SD	●		●		●	●
TN						
TX			●		●	●
UT						
VT			●			●
VA			●			●
WA		●	●		●	●
WV			●			●
WI			●		●	●
WY			●		●	

Appendix II

$\blacklozenge$

Gaming Directory by State

State Regulatory Agencies	Web Site
Birmingham, Alabama Racing Commission	www.mindspring.com/~brc
Alaska Dept. of Revenue Gaming Unit	www.tax.state.ak.us/divisions/gaming.htm
Arizona Department of Gaming	www.gm.state.az.us
Arkansas Racing Commission	www.state.ar.us/directory
California Horse Racing Board	www.chrb.ca.gov
Colorado Division of Gaming	www.gaming.state.co.us
Colorado Division of Racing Events	www.revenue.state.co.us
Connecticut Division of Special Revenue	www.dosr.state.ct.us
Delaware Thoroughbred Racing Commission	www.state.de.us.deptagri/index.htm
Florida Division of Pari-Mutuel Wagering	www.myflorida.com/dpbr/pmw/index.shtml
Idaho State Racing Commission	www.isp.state.id.us/race
Illinois Racing Board	www.state.il.us/agency/irb
Illinois Gaming Board	www.igb.state.il.us
Iowa Department of Inspections and Appeals	www.state.ia.us/government/dia
Iowa Division of Criminal Investigation Gaming Bureau (Race and River Gaming)	www.state.ia.us/government/dps/dci/ gaming.htm

Source: The Digital Daily; www.irs.gov/business/small. May 14, 2002.

State Regulatory Agencies	Web Site
Iowa Racing and Gaming Commission	www.state.ia.us/igrc
Kansas State Gaming Agency	www.ink.org/public/ksga
Kansas Racing and Gaming Commission	www.ink.org/public/ksga
Kentucky Racing Commission	www.state.ky.us/agencies/cppr/krcl
Louisiana Gaming Control Board	www.dps.state.la.us/lgcb
Maryland Racing Commission	www.dllr.state.md.us/racing/
Massachusetts State Racing Commission	www.state.ma.us/src/
Michigan Office of the Racing Commissioner	www.mda.state.mi.us/racing
Michigan Gaming Control Board	www.michigan.gov/mgcb
Minnesota DPS Alcohol and Gambling Enforcement Division	www.dps.state.mn.us/alcgamb
Minnesota Racing Commission	www.state.mn.us/ebranch/racing
Mississippi Gaming Commission	www.mgc.state.ms.us
Missouri Gaming Commission	www.mgc.state.mo.us
Montana DOJ Gambling Control	www.doj.state.mt.us/gcd
Nevada Gaming Commission and Gaming Control Board	www.gaming.state.nv.us
New Hampshire Pari-Mutuel Commission	www.webster.state.nh.us.nhpmc
New Jersey Casino Control Commission	www.state.nj.us/casinos/index.html
New Jersey Division of Gaming Enforcement	www.state.nj.us/lps/ge
New Mexico Alcohol and Gaming Division	www.rld.state.nm.us/agd/index.html
New Mexico Racing Commission	http://nmrc.state.nm.us

State Regulatory Agencies	Web Site
New York State Racing and Wagering Board	www.racing.state.ny.us
North Dakota AG Gaming Commission	www.ag.state.nd.us
Oklahoma Horse Racing Commission	www.ohrc.state.ok.us
Oregon Racing Commission	www.orednet.org
Pennsylvania Horse & Harness Racing Commissions	Sites.state.pa.us/PA_Exec/Agriculture/commissions/horse_harness
Rhode Island Department of Business Regulation	www.dbr.state.ri.us
South Carolina Department of Revenue	www.sctax.org
South Dakota Commission on Gaming	www.state.sd.us/dcr/gaming
Texas Racing Commission	www.txrc.state.tx.us
Virginia Racing commission	www.vrc.state.va.us
Washington State Gambling Commission	www.wsgc.wa.gov
West Virginia Racing Commission	www.state.wv.us/racing
Wisconsin Division of Gaming	www.doa.state.wi.us/gaming/racing
Wyoming Pari-Mutuel Commission	Parimutuel.state.wy.us

Gaming Associations	
The International Association of Gaming Regulators	www.iagr.org
National Indian Gaming Association	www.indiangaming.org

Federal Government	*Web Site*
National Indian Gaming Commission	www.nigc.gov
U.S. Treasury-Financial Crimes Enforcement Network (FinCen)	www.ustreas.gov/fincen

Appendix III

◆

Gaming Withholding and Reporting Requirements

GAMING WITHHOLDING AND REPORTING THRESHOLDS

Specific Games	Form 1099 Required	Form W-2G Proceeds Not Reduced by Wager	Form W-2G Proceeds Reduced by Wager	Form W-2G Withholding Required (1)	Form 1042-S Foreign Payouts Verifiable Payments (2)	Excise Tax (Based on the Wager)
Slot Win		$1,200			Yes	No
Bingo		$1,200			Yes	No
Keno Win (1–20 Games)			$1,500		Yes	No
Keno Wins (over 20 games)			$1,500		Yes	Yes
Sweepstakes, Lotteries, Wagering Pools (proceeds more than 300 times the amount wagered)			$600		Yes	Yes (State conducted lotteries are exempt)
Sweepstakes, Lotteries, Wagering Pools. Withholding required regardless of payout odds				$5,000	Yes	Yes (State conducted lotteries are exempt

(1) Winnings must be reduced by the amount wagered and the proceeds must exceed $5,000.

(2) Payments made to nonresident aliens are subject to withholding and reporting on Form 1042-S (proceeds from Blackjack, Craps, Roulette, Baccarat, or Big Wheel 6 are exempt).

Source: The Digital Daily; www.irs.gov/business/small. May 14, 2002.

Specific Games	Form 1099 Required	Form W-2G Proceeds Not Reduced by Wager	Form W-2G Proceeds Reduced by Wager	Form W-2G Withholding Required (1)	Form 1042-S Foreign Payouts Verifiable Payments (2)	Excise Tax (Based on the Wager)
Wagering transaction with proceeds more than 300 times the amount wagered (3)			$600	$5,000	Yes	No
Tournament— no entry fee (4)	$600				Yes	No
Pari-Mutuel, including horse racing, dog racing, jai alai, with proceeds more than 300 times the amount wagered			$600	$5,000	Yes	No
Prizes received with no wager (Drawings, Promotions, etc.)	$600				Yes	No
Sports event or contest (only reportable if proceeds exceed 300 times the wager)			$600	$5,000	Yes	Yes

(3) Players of these table games can receive payments where the proceeds exceed 300 times the wager. These payments are subject to reporting at $600 in proceeds and withholding is applicable at $5,000 in proceeds.

(4) Tournaments with entry fees must be analyzed to see if the entry fee is a wager, and if the proceeds exceed the wager by 300 times or more, or if the tournament is a wagering pool.

BACKUP WITHHOLDING

You must withhold 30 percent of certain taxable payments if the payee fails to furnish you with his or her correct taxpayer identification number (TIN). This withholding is referred to as "backup withholding."

Appendix IV

◆

Gaming Tax Calendar

Form	Name of Form	Purpose of Form	Period Covered	Due Date
Form 1099	Miscellaneous Income	Prizes and awards that are not for services performed. Include the fair market value of merchandise. Also include amounts paid to a winner of a sweepstakes not involving a wager.	Specific date of prize or award	February 28 (Paper or magnetic media) April 1 (Electronically)
Form W-2G	Certain Gambling Winnings	To report gambling winnings and any federal withholding on the winnings.	Jackpot date	February 28 (Paper or magnetic media) April 1 (Electronically)
Form 5754	Statement by Person(s) Receiving Gambling Win	When the person receiving gambling winnings subject to reporting or withholding is not the actual winner, or is a member of a group of two or more winners on the same winning ticket.	Jackpot date	February 28 (Paper or magnetic media) April 1 (Electronically)
Form 730	Tax on Wagering	You must file this form and pay the tax on wagers under section 4401 (a) if you: —Are in the business of accepting wagers, —Conducting a wagering pool or lottery, or	Monthly	By last day of the following month

Source: The Digital Daily; www.irs.gov/business. May 14, 2002.

Form	Name of Form	Purpose of Form	Period Covered	Due Date
Form 730 (cont.)		—Are required to be registered and you receive wagers for or on behalf of another person, but do not register that person's name and address.		
Form W-7	Application for IRS individual Taxpayer Identification Number (ITIN)	An ITIN is a nine-digit number issued by the U.S. Internal Revenue Service to individuals who are required to have a U.S. taxpayer identification number, but who do not have and are not eligible to obtain a Social Security number.	No specific period	No due date
Form W-9	Request for Taxpayer Identification Number and Certification	To request the taxpayer identification number (ITIN) of a U.S. person (including a resident alien) and to request certain certifications and claims for exemption.	No specific period	No due date
Form 8300	Report of Cash Payments over $10,000 Received in a Trade or Business	Each person engaged in a trade or business who, in the course of that trade or business, received more than $10,000 in cash in one transaction or in two or more related transactions must file Form 8300.	Day cash received	By the 15th day after the date the cash was received

Form	Name of Form	Purpose of Form	Period Covered	Due Date
Form 8362	Currency Transaction Report by Casinos	To report each transaction involving either currency received (Cash In) or currency disbursed (Cash Out) of more than $10,000 in a gaming day. (Who Must File: Any organization duly licensed or authorized to do business as a casino or gambling casino in the United States—except casinos located in Nevada—see Form 8852, and having gross annual gaming revenues in excess of $1 million must file Form 8362. This includes the principle headquarters and every domestic branch or place of business of the casino.)	Transaction date	File each Form 8362 by the 15th calendar day after the day of the transaction
Form 8852	Currency Transaction Report by Casinos—Nevada	To report a transaction that involves more than $10,000 in cash or smaller transactions occurring within a designated 24-hour period that aggregate to more than $10,000 cash.	Transaction date	File each Form 8852 by the 15th calendar day after the day of the transaction.

Appendix V

◆

Internal Revenue Service—Publication 529

Miscellaneous Deductions: Gambling Losses Up to the Amount of Gambling Winnings

You must report the full amount of your gambling winnings for the year on line 21, Form 1040. You deduct your gambling losses for the year on line 27, Schedule A (Form 1040). You cannot deduct gambling losses that are more than your winnings.

You cannot reduce your gambling winnings by your gambling losses and report the difference. You must report the full amount of your winnings as income and claim your losses (up to the amount of winnings) as an itemized deduction. Therefore, your records show your winnings separately from your losses.

Diary of winnings and losses. You must keep an accurate diary or similar record of your losses and winnings. Your diary should contain at least the following information.

1. The date and type of your specific wager or wagering activity.
2. The name and address or location of the gambling establishment.
3. The names of other persons present with you at the gambling establishment.
4. The amount(s) you won or lost.

Proof of winnings and losses. In addition to your diary, you should also have other documentation. You can generally prove your winnings and losses through Form W-2G, Certain *Gambling Winnings*, Form 5754, *Statement by Person(s) Receiving Gambling Winnings*, wagering tickets, cancelled checks, credit records, bank withdrawals, and statements of actual winnings or payment slips provided to you by the gambling establishment.

For specific wagering transactions, you can use the following items to support your winnings and losses.

Keno: Copies of the keno tickets you purchased that were validated by the gambling establishment, copies of your casino credit records, and copies of your casino check-cashing records.

Slot machines: A record of the machine number and all winnings by date and time the machine was played.

Table games (twenty-one, blackjack, craps, poker, baccarat, roulette, wheel of fortune, etc.): The number of the table at which you were playing. Casino credit card data indicating whether the credit was issued in the pit or at the cashier's cage.

Bingo: A record of the number of games played, cost of tickets purchased, and amounts collected on winning tickets. Supplemental records include any receipts from the casino, parlor, etc.

Racing (horse, harness, dog, etc.): A record of the races, amounts of wagers, amounts collected on winning tickets, and amounts lost on losing tickets. Supplemental records include unredeemed tickets and payment records from the racetrack.

Lotteries: A record of ticket purchases, dates, winnings, and losses. Supplemental records include unredeemed tickets, payment slips, and winnings statements.

These record-keeping suggestions are intended as general guidelines to help you establish your winnings and losses. They are not all-inclusive. Your tax liability depends on your particular facts and circumstances.

Appendix VI

◆

Internal Revenue Service— Tax Topic 419: Gambling Income and Expenses

Gambling winnings are fully taxable and must be reported on your tax return. You must file Form 1040 and include all of your winnings on line 21. Gambling income includes, but is not limited to, winnings from lotteries, raffles, horse races, and casinos. It includes not only cash winnings, but also the fair market value of prizes such as cars and trips. For additional information, refer to Publication 525, *Taxable and Nontaxable Income*.

If you receive $600 or more in gambling winnings, the payer generally is required to issue you a Form W-2G. If you have won more than $5,000, the payer generally is required to withhold 27 percent of the proceeds for Federal Income Tax. If you did not provide your Social Security Number, the payer may have to withhold 30 percent. For more information on withholding, refer to Publication 505, *Tax Withholding and Estimated Tax*.

You can deduct gambling losses only if you itemize deductions. Claim your gambling losses as a miscellaneous deduction on Schedule A Form 1040, line 27. However, the amount of losses you deduct cannot be more than the amount of gambling income you have reported on your return. It is important to keep an accurate diary or similar record of your gambling winnings and losses. To deduct your losses, you must be able to provide receipts, tickets, statements, or other records that show the amount of both your winnings and losses. Refer to Publication 529, *Miscellaneous Deductions*, for more information.

Conclusion

Tax situations are very unique for gaming enthusiasts, and gambling activity requires constant monitoring and documenting. Proper planning is needed on a continuing basis to avoid unwanted tax surprises. Unfortunately, there's no way to avoid the possibility of having your tax return selected for an IRS review. But at least there is comfort and security in knowing that all necessary reporting requirements have been met. As always, consult your accountant or tax adviser with any questions you may have.

References and Resources

GAMING REFERENCES

Bargain City
by Anthony Curtis
Huntington Press
Order yours today!
1-800-244-2224

Harrah's Survey of Casino Entertainment 1995 & 1996
Harrah's Marketing Communications
1023 Cherry Road
Memphis, TN 38117

TAX REFERENCES

CCH Standard Federal Tax Reported
by CCH Tax Law Editors
Commerce Clearing House, Inc.
4025 West Peterson Avenue
Chicago, IL 60646

Internal Revenue Code of 1986

The 2002 Form 1040 Tax Package
Forms and Instructions
Department of the Treasury
Internal Revenue Service
P.O. Box 8905
Bloomington, IL 61702

Publication 525
Taxable and Nontaxable Income
Department of the Treasury
Internal Revenue Service
Cat. No 15047D

Publication 529
Miscellaneous Deductions
Department of the Treasury
Internal Revenue Service
Cat. No. 15056O

The Digital Daily
www.irs.gov

J.K. Lasser's Your Income Tax 2002
Professional Edition
Prepared by J.K. Lasser Institute
Fifty-eighth edition
Macmillan General Reference
A Prentice Hall Macmillan Company
15 Columbus Circle
New York, NY 10023

RIA's Analysis of Federal Taxes
Copyright 1995 by Research Institute of America
90 Fifth Avenue
New York, NY 10011

The Wall Street Journal
200 Liberty Street
New York, NY 10281

TRAVEL AND TOURISM REFERENCES

Atlantic City Convention & Visitors Authority
2314 Pacific Avenue
Atlantic City, NJ 08401
(609) 449-7122

Las Vegas Convention & Visitors Authority
3150 Paradise Road
Las Vegas, NV 89109
(702) 892-0711

Index

situation 1, 50–55
situation 2, 56–61
State(s). *See also specific states*
gaming activities by, 135–36
gaming directory by, 137–41
State income taxes, lottery winnings
and, 85–86, 88
Statute of Anne (1710), 76–77
Student Athlete Protection Act, 72
Study on impact of gambling, 67–70
Substantiated losses, 7, 9, 11
Cohan Rule and, 47–48
lottery winnings and, 86–87
Revenue Procedure 77–29 and, 28,
29–32
Super Bowl wagers, 101, 102
Surveillance systems, 109
Suspicious Activity Reports—Casinos
(SARCs), 117
Sweepstakes, 94, 95
withholding and reporting
requirements, 100, 143
Szkirczak v. Commissioner, 10

Table games, record keeping, 11, 32,
152
Tax calendar, 147–49
Tax Court
comps and, 16–17
professional gamblers and, 21–23
use of estimates and, 46–47
Tax frauds, 99–100, 104
Tax rates, 24–25, 97
Tax references, 157–58
Tax Topic 419, 153
Temperance movement, 78
Tennessee, gaming activities, 136
Texas
gaming activities, 136
regulatory agencies, 140
Theft, 108–9
Thorson, Kenneth W., 121
Tips (tokes), 13
defined, 132
Tourist information, 158–59

Tournament play, 82, 92–93, 99
"Trade or business," 21–23
Tribal gaming, defined, 132–33

Unlawful Internet Gambling Funding
Prohibition Act, 70–71
Unofficial Guide to Casino Gambling
(Nestor), 80, 108–9
Use of estimates, 45–46
Utah, gaming activities, 136

Vermont, gaming activities, 136
Virginia
gaming activities, 136
regulatory agencies, 141

Wade, Nathan L., 125
Wagering tickets, 29, 31
Wagers, defined, 133
Wally the Winner, 3–5
Washington
gaming activities, 136
regulatory agencies, 141
Washington, George, 77–78
West Virginia
gaming activities, 136
regulatory agencies, 141
Winkler v. United States, 10
Winnings, use of term, 6. *See also*
Income
Wisconsin
gaming activities, 136
regulatory agencies, 141
Withholding, 92, 98–99, 113–14
lottery winnings and, 87–88
for nonresident aliens, 98–99
requirements for reporting, 100,
143–45
Write offs, of gambling losses, 6–7
W-2G. *See* Form W-2G
Wyoming
gaming activities, 136
regulatory agencies, 141

Zielonka, John David, 45–47

About the Author

Walter L. Lewis, CPA

Walt is one of the founding partners of Smith, Lewis, Chess & Company, a CPA firm with two offices in southwestern Pennsylvania. He is a current member of both the Pennsylvania and the American Institute of Certified Public Accountants. He earned a B.S. in business management with a concentration in accounting from Indiana University of Pennsylvania (IUP). His thirty years' experience, along with his respected financial opinions, have earned him positions on the advisory boards of numerous institutions and privately held corporations. He takes great pride in being able to present complicated tax issues in an understandable way.